cooking up a storm

Sam Stern
and Susan Stern, who got him started

WALKER BOOKS
AND SUBSIDIARIES
LONDON · BOSTON · SYDNEY · AUCKLAND

contents

I've written this book for kids like me who enjoy cooking or who are keen to learn to cook. It's full of simple tasty recipes – the sort of things that my mates and I like to eat...

You'll find the full whack of food in here. From snacks that you can wolf down while you're watching The Simpsons through to some full-on dishes that you can serve up to your family.

Cooking's a particular challenge in our house. I'm the youngest of five kids. One of my sisters is a veggie. Another is an ex-veggie who won't eat red meat. My brother's a meat freak. My dad's a bit of a garbage can but he can't eat chocolate or cheese – his favourite foods. My mum won't eat anything that's tough on her teeth. Me? I eat anything but bananas and broccoli. So catering for everyone means that there's a wide range of food that has to get served up. It's those everyday foods that I've learned to cook. And that's where I've got this book full of recipes. There's food here for all tastes. There's what I call "big" food – the stuff that you want when you've been doing loads of sport – you're mega-hungry and want some real eating. There's brain food – treats to get the brain cells and the tastebuds up and the nerves soothed down when you've got exams. And there's food you can eat if you know you've got a bit of a sofa habit but you don't want to end up like a sofa. There's food here to keep you fit and to keep you looking fit. And there's party food when you'll want to put on some spectacular eating.

Why do I like cooking? Well, I'm usually pretty impatient but I can spend hours chopping stuff, blitzing, whisking and mixing. I find all that activity's really relaxing. First off I get into the kitchen and put on some music. I love all the technical stuff that goes with cooking. Learning the basics – like how to make batters, pastry, bread, sauces, soups. Doing it the way that it says in the book and then when I'm confident, getting more creative – ignoring how Mum does it – doing it my way. You have to take charge when you're cooking. Use your judgement.

I like the fact that when you're cooking you're using your senses. The feel of pastry, the smell of melting chocolate and fresh bread. There's the sound of a fry-up or popcorn exploding. I like it that you're in touch with your food when you do things yourself. You make your own choices. Real cooking is hands on. Not just opening the freezer and grabbing a pizza.

Cooking even makes shopping kind of OK. I used to hate shopping for food till I started cooking. But now it's a mission to search out the best ingredients. Me and my mum often go as a team. There's a real art to it. Did you know that you can tell if a fruit is ready to eat by touching or sniffing it? Or that there are signs to look out for which tell you if meat's going to be tender or rip your teeth out? Or that you can tell how fresh a fish is by looking it straight in the eye? I love all that. If there's a rule to shopping I guess it's that the best sort of

cooking comes from the freshest ingredients. So sort out the supermarket that suits you best. Find your nearest good market and specialist shop. Don't eat rubbish. It's the number one rule. Food has to deserve to be eaten.

I like to know where my food's from. My old farmer grandad used to say "you are what you eat". He grew everything he ate and was active and healthy till he was really old. And as I am what I eat then I think I've got the right to know as much as possible about what I'm eating.

What do I like to eat? Chocolate mousse … lemony roast chicken with all the trimmings … chocolate roulade … spaghetti Bolognese with garlic bread … everything that's tapas … onion soup with floating cheese toasts … sweet potato

roasties … guacamole … chickpea, spinach and potato curry … garlic roast veg … the ultimate crunch bacon sandwich… The variety of things that you can cook is just amazing. And it's so easy to do. One minute you can be standing in your kitchen thinking to yourself, I'm hungry – what shall I cook? – and then a couple of hours later you can have all your family or your mates sitting round a table eating a real feast that you've made yourself. Or you're just in from school and there's no-one about. So you make yourself up some pasta with a tasty tomato sauce. Takes you ten minutes tops from thinking it to having it hot and steamy and delicious there on a plate. Cooking's never boring. Once you can do it you'll always do it. It's brilliant to know you can be independent.

Many adults these days don't like to cook, don't know how to cook or don't have the time to cook, which is a bit of a shame cos they're missing out. Maybe they didn't get the chance to learn when they were our age. If this is your parents, get your cooking sorted and then do them a really big favour – teach them.

None of these recipes is tricky. Some are easy – some are really easy. Some are fast – some take a bit of time. (Make some of them in advance.) And if you're big eaters in your house, use my quantities (then you won't need to snack.) If you're a smaller eater cut them down. If you've been on a cookery course or you cook at home, you won't have any trouble getting them down. And if you're a first time cook then don't worry. Just follow the recipes. Good luck and get cooking.

Brilliant breakfasts

Getting up can be a real pain (particularly on a school day) but there are compensations. **Breakfast!**

This is the meal that gets me up and then sets me up for the day. Even if I don't think I want it, the smell of the bacon gets those juices going. Sometimes it's got to be something pretty damn quick – Dad's barking at me to get my teeth done – have I got my books, my sports gear? I'm late again. But I still want something tasty and nutritious. I love **toast**. With just about anything on it. **Eggs** done any way. A **juicy hot grapefruit** for a cold day. A **yogurt and fruit mix**. Maybe a **smoothie**.

Holidays and weekends – it's a whole different story (and a bit of a lie-in with any luck) so there's more time to put something special together. **Pancakes**, **drop scones**, a post-sleepover **fry-up**, or maybe my all time favourite **tomato bruschetta**. Get some cool cooking done and ditch the sackfuls of cereals.

Eggs

When we had chickens at the bottom of the garden we'd eat their eggs. Free-range organic birds produce eggs with a rich orange yolk and an amazing taste. Now the birds have gone we have to buy them. When you buy them, make sure they're fresh. Eggs make a great breakfast food – boiled, poached, scrambled, fried. They build muscle, so get cooking them if you're into your sport. The protein in them is great for your brain. Enjoy them in your favourite fast way. Or maybe save yourself for a holiday or weekend omelette.

For 1
Ingredients
1–2 eggs at room
   temperature
Salt

Eat with: Vegemite and butter on toast soldiers.

For 1
Ingredients
1 fresh egg
Buttered toast
Salt and black pepper

Boiled egg

A cracking start to the day (I know uni students who can't do it).

Method
1. Bring a small saucepan two-thirds full of water to the boil. Add a little salt. Use a spoon to lower the eggs into the pan.
2. Bring back to the boil. Set the timer for 4 minutes (soft) or 5 minutes (medium). Or 6 minutes if eggs straight from fridge.

Perfect poached egg

You can buy a poacher for this but you don't need it. Rely on a steady hand and a bit of science!

Method
1. Two-thirds fill a small saucepan or frying pan with water. Add a pinch of salt and bring to the boil.
2. Turn the heat down a smidge. Crack the egg into a cup.
3. Use a wooden spoon to stir the water, creating a whirlpool

effect. Slip the egg down into the centre of the whirling water (this keeps the egg white together in a neat shape).

4. Simmer gently for 3–4 minutes until the white is set.

5. When the egg is done, lift it out gently with a slotted spoon (or fish slice if cooking in a frying pan). Drain well.

6. Set on buttered toast and add a twist of black pepper.

VARIATION

Put dressed salad leaves on a toasted English muffin. Perch a poached egg and crisp bacon rasher on top for a great brunch.

Scrambled eggs

Making perfect scrambled eggs is like getting to the next level on a tricky PS2 game. You need a good eye and well-fast reflexes. Cook the eggs for too long and they end up dry and clumpy. Stop the exact second before they're ready – they'll be softer and sweeter.

For 1
Ingredients

2 eggs
Knob of butter
Buttered toast
Salt and black pepper

Eat with: Grilled tomatoes, mushrooms and bacon on the side.

Method

1. Crack the eggs into a bowl. Beat well with a fork. Season.

2. Melt the butter in a small saucepan on low heat. Tip in eggs and stir like mad with a wooden spoon for 1–2 minutes as they cook, making sure the egg doesn't stick to the pan.

3. Take off the heat while the eggs are still soft. Keep stirring for a few seconds. Chuck onto your toast. Eat now.

VARIATION

At STEP 3, toss in any of the following: grated cheese; chopped parsley, chives or tarragon; finely diced tomato and a pinch of sugar; diced cooked ham; crumbled crisp bacon; diced fried chorizo sausage; diced smoked salmon.

For 1
Ingredients
50 g/2 oz porridge oats
300 ml/½ pint water or
  milk and water mixed
Salt

Eat with: Milk, cream or Greek-style yogurt.

Brown sugar, honey or maple syrup.

Or add a dollop of spiced apple puree. Here's how: chop up a peeled and cored cooking apple or two. Cook in a pan on a gentle heat with a little water, a sprinkle of cinnamon and sugar until you've a good smooth puree. Keep in the fridge till you need it.

VARIATION
At STEP 3 add a few fresh raspberries or blueberries.

Porridge

I sometimes eat this before I go off on an all-day trip. Maybe paint-balling or fishing. The energy in the oats keeps me going. And it's quick to make. Just as well – it gives me loads more time to sort my equipment. OK it's kind of gloopy, but mixed with the right stuff I really like it.

Method
1. Put the oats with water (or milk and water) in a small pan.
2. Heat to boiling, stirring continuously. Reduce heat and simmer, stirring for 4 minutes, till thick, smooth and creamy.
3. Add a pinch of salt and stir. Serve.

Hot sugared pink grapefruit

This one can drag you out from under the duvet – even on cold, dark mornings when school looms. Heating fruit makes the juices flow, even with stuff that's been hanging around for a bit. So sprinkle your fruit with a bit of sugar and flash grill it.

Method

1. Preheat your grill on maximum.
2. Cut the grapefruit in half.
3. Using a grapefruit or vegetable knife cut the fruit into loose segments so you'll be able to spoon the flesh out easily with a teaspoon.
4. Sprinkle the top of each with a little sugar.
5. Balance the grapefruit on the rack of your grill pan.
6. Stick under the heat for up to 2 minutes – the top should be sizzling and the fruit warmed right through.

For 1

Ingredients

1 pink grapefruit
1 teaspoon sugar (brown or white to taste)

Eat with: Wholemeal toast for a complete breakfast.

WHY NOT?

Prepare a grapefruit and an orange as STEP 3. Throw in a bowl. Sprinkle with a little caster sugar and cinnamon (if you like spice). Let it sit for a bit if you've got time. Chop some seedless grapes in half and chuck those in.

Field mushrooms on toast

For 1

Ingredients

3 large field or 8 button
  mushrooms
Knob of butter
Light olive oil
1–2 slices bread
Salt and black pepper
Lemon

Eat with: My mum's treacle bread, toasted, to give a lovely sweet edge to the taste (page 152).

I didn't think much of mushrooms until I discovered this little dish. But field mushrooms have real character. Big in size and dark in taste. Why are they called field mushrooms? My grandad used to search the fields at five in the morning for them, so I guess that's the reason.

Method

1. Peel your mushrooms: find a loose edge and using your fingers just peel away until the mushroom looks naked. If you're using buttons, wash and blot them dry on kitchen paper.
2. Cut off stems, then slice the mushrooms across quite thickly.
3. Heat a frying pan, add butter and a glug of light olive oil. The oil tastes good, is better for you and stops butter burning. Don't use too much. Mushrooms soak up the grease. It's better to top up the oil if your fungi are looking too dry.
4. Use a fish slice or spatula to turn the mushrooms as they cook so you catch each surface.
5. When they're almost done, stick the bread in the toaster.
6. Season your mushrooms. They'll just be shedding some of their lovely juices into the pan by now. So sprinkle on some sea salt. Add black pepper if you like it. You can squeeze a bit of lemon juice over.
7. Pile the mushrooms on hot toast and pour on the juices. Lovely!

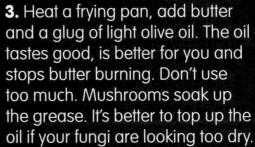

Serves 1
Ingredients

SOFT BERRY SMOOTHIE
150 ml/5 fl oz natural
  or low-fat yogurt
Handful of blueberries
Handful of raspberries
1 teaspoon honey

**STRAWBERRY AND
BANANA SMOOTHIE**
150 ml/5 fl oz natural
  yogurt, low-fat yogurt
  or skimmed milk
Handful of strawberries
1 banana, chopped
1 teaspoon honey

WHY NOT?
Use any soft fruit
combos. Don't like
honey? Use some fresh
apple or orange juice
instead.
Did you know that
eating blueberries
helps to boost your IQ?

Two fruit smoothies

Running late for school? Feeling a bit rubbish? Have yourself a smoothie. They're, like, multi-task type foods. Quick and perfect when you're not in the mood for traditional eating. The fruit and yogurt combo gives you the right brain energy to help with concentration as well as the nutrients to help out with sport. I sometimes use a hand-held blender. Saves on the washing up. Try out these two fruity numbers, then get creative – sort your own favourites.

Method

1. Put the ingredients into a blender. Whizz till smooth. Alternatively, use a hand-held blender. Put the ingredients into a plastic jug or deep bowl and blitz everything till smooth.
2. Taste. Add more fruit or honey if you think it needs it.
3. Serve with or without straws.

For 1
Ingredients

2 rashers really
 good bacon
Butter
2 slices fresh white
 bread
2 thin slices tomato
Dollop of brown sauce
 (you can use ketchup)

VARIATION

⭐ Add a fried egg
and another layer of
bread to make a
breakfast club
sandwich.

⭐ Skip the bread
and eat in a muffin.

Classic bacon sandwich

The smell of this beauty is almost enough to turn a vegetarian into a full-on carnivore. It happened to my mum and one of my sisters. This makes a great pre-school eat. And we always have it when mates stay over. Lovely crisp grilled bacon matched with a slice or two of cool tomato. I always use white bread – either thin sliced or thick crusty. It's not quite the same on brown. And good old brown sauce. For some, this classic sandwich is seventh heaven.

Method

1. Preheat the grill to maximum.
2. Line the grill pan with foil. Place the bacon rashers on the rack in the pan.
3. Grill the bacon till it's as crisp as you like on both sides.
4. Spread a thin layer of butter on the bread.
5. Make a sandwich with bacon, tomato and sauce.

Mashed banana & yogurt bowl

I have to confess I can't get my head around bananas. I know they're good for you and everyone else seems to go mad for them. But I'm not there yet. Anyway this recipe is for all you banana lovers out there. Like my sister Poll. Who can't get enough of them. When we go to visit my granny in Suffolk she always gives her a mashed banana for breakfast. It's a family tradition. My mum works in the theatre. So if she's got a busy day ahead with her actors she'll often eat this dish to get her off to a good start. She says that actors love bananas. They use so much energy in rehearsals that they keep them going. And I swear I've seen tennis players eating them to boost their games. Who knows? Maybe I'll grow into them. This breakfast dish is sooo easy. And there are loads of nutrients in there to power you through your drama and tennis!

For 2
Ingredients
2 bananas
300 ml/½ pint natural yogurt, preferably Greek-style
Runny honey (optional)

VARIATION
⭐ Layer yogurt and banana with raspberries and crunchy cereal in a tall glass.

⭐ Crush blueberries into the yogurt instead of banana.

⭐ Chuck in walnuts and raisins, swirl with honey or maple syrup.

⭐ Peel and chop some orange. Layer with honeyed yogurt and crumbled biscuit.

Method
1. Mash your banana roughly (or chop if you prefer chunks).
2. Tip yogurt into bowl.
3. Chuck banana into yogurt and stir.
4. Add any extra bits to suit your fancy.
5. Drizzle a bit of honey over the top to taste.
6. Eat immediately.

Makes 8

Ingredients

100 g/4 oz plain flour
Pinch of salt
1 egg
300 ml/½ pint milk
Butter for cooking

Eat with:

SWEET: Maple syrup,
freshly squeezed lemon
or orange juice, and
sugar.

SAVOURY: Grated cheese
and cooked ham.

Pancakes

Fancy a bit of early morning juggling? Then try pancakes. These treats tick all the boxes. They're tasty, popular, quick to prepare and make easy eating. Team them with whatever extras take your fancy. If you like, make your mix the night before. Store in the fridge in your measuring jug. Just before you're ready to cook, give the mix a couple of good whisks with a fork. Now it's ready to pour into your pan. Warning: the first pancake of the batch often sticks and needs chucking away. If this happens to you, you're not a failure.

Method

1. Sift the flour and salt into a bowl. Make a deep dent in the flour. Crack the egg and drop it into this hole.
2. Tip a good glug of the milk on to the unbeaten egg. With your wooden spoon, start to beat the egg and milk together in a circular movement without mixing in too much flour at first.
3. Gradually mix in the rest of the flour and start to beat everything furiously. Hold on to the bowl with one hand as you do this. Tip the bowl to one side slightly if it helps. The aim is to build up some real wrist action to make sure that the batter becomes smooth while it's still very thick.
4. Add the rest of the milk bit by bit, beating until you have a lovely smooth thin batter. If it's not entirely smooth you can always use a balloon whisk to blitz those blobs out.
5. Heat a pancake pan or small frying pan. You want it hot enough to make the butter sizzle when you chuck it in.
6. Use a little knob of butter to coat the pan very lightly. If the butter starts to go brown it's beginning to burn and starts to taste bitter, so whip the pan off the heat if this happens.
7. Pour 2–3 tablespoons batter into your pan and swirl it round immediately so that it coats the entire surface.

8. Now cook until you think the underside is done. Check by flicking up the edge of the pancake with your spatula. If it's cooked it is lightly browned and it doesn't stick.

9. Tossing time. Or play it safe and use a fish slice or spatula to turn the pancake over.

10. Cook second side till light brown and serve immediately.

VARIATION

At STEP 6, toss a handful of blueberries into the pan till they're softening and oozing juices, then pour in batter mix. Cook. Don't toss – turn with a spatula.

Makes 12
Ingredients
225 g/8 oz self-raising
  flour
Pinch salt
1 tablespoon caster
  sugar
2 eggs
300 ml/½ pint milk
25–50 g/1–2 oz butter,
  melted

Eat with:

SWEET: Honey, golden
syrup, peanut butter,
maple syrup or butter and
jam.

SAVOURY: Cream cheese
and smoked salmon.
Crisp cooked bacon and
maple syrup.

Drop scones

If you're down with pancakes then you're ninety-nine
per cent of the way to drop scones. The recipe's close
but the method's quite different. (We had to text it to
my brother at uni to make for his mates.) Eat these
warm. Pile them high with excellent flavours.

Method

1. Sift the flour, salt and sugar into a bowl. Make a deep dent in
the flour mixture. Add the eggs and a little milk.
2. Use a wooden spoon to beat the egg and milk, gradually
mixing in the flour, as for pancakes (page 18). Mix till all the milk
is used to make a smooth thicker batter.
3. Use a pastry brush to brush melted butter on to a large
heavy frying pan. Heat the pan on medium heat.
4. Drop a tablespoon of the batter on to the hot pan. Repeat,
leaving room between them.
5. Cook for a couple of minutes until the surface breaks into
bubbles and the bottoms are just browned.
6. Flick over with a spatula. Cook other side.
7. Spread scones on a tea towel. Cover to keep warm.

For 4
Ingredients

450 g/1 lb plums
250 ml/8 fl oz water
3 tablespoons sugar or
  to taste
1 vanilla pod or 1
  teaspoon natural
  vanilla extract

Eat with: Natural yogurt
or porridge, warm or
cold.

VARIATION
Add fresh apricots,
nectarines, peaches
or blueberries.

Baked vanilla plums

We've got plum trees in the garden so if it's a good
crop we've got to find lots of different ways of using
them. Throwing them isn't popular. Here they're
baked with a vanilla pod – which looks a bit like
something the cat's brought in. Slit the pod with a
sharp knife to release the flavour and let it bake with
the plums. These really sharpen you up if you eat
them for breakfast. Wash the pod
and let it dry on a bit of kitchen paper,
so you can re-use it next time.

Method

1. Preheat the oven to 200°C/400°F/gas 6.
2. Cut the plums in half and remove their
stones if you wish or leave whole. Stick them
in a shallow baking dish with the water and
sugar. Add a little more water if needed.
3. Slit the pod and throw it in or add the
vanilla extract. Cover with a lid or foil.
4. Bake for 30 minutes, until the plums are
soft and starting to break up.

For 1
Ingredients

Light olive oil
1 favourite sausage
1 slice bread, cut in half
  into 2 triangles
1 big fat tomato, halved
2 rindless rashers good-
  quality back bacon
2 slices black pudding
  (optional)
1 flat mushroom or 3–4
  button mushrooms
1 egg

Eat with: Baked beans.
Heat through gently.

VARIATION

Try it in a sandwich:
Grill the bacon and
tomatoes. Lightly fry
the mushrooms.
Poach an egg. Grill a
piece of Italian
ciabatta or focaccia.
Pile on the tomato
and mushroom, then
the crisp bacon
rasher. Top with the
poached egg.

All-day breakfast fry-up

Otherwise known as Full English Breakfast. Because that's how you feel after you've eaten it. I never fancy this on a school day, but if I'm getting up late after a late night and have time to enjoy what I'm eating, then this is the one I'll often go for. I like a good mix of textures and flavours: crisp fried bread and bacon, soft juicy tomato. I like a slice or two of black pudding. If you're an egg fan, then go for it. Go over the top with some tasty mushrooms.

Method

1. Preheat the oven to 200°C/400°F/gas 6.
2. Stick the sausage in a baking tray to cook for 20 minutes.
3. Wait ten minutes. Heat frying pan and drizzle in a little oil.
4. Throw in the bread. Cook one side till crisp then turn over and brown the second side. Drain on kitchen paper, put on breakfast plate and keep warm.
5. Add a drop of oil to the pan and fry the tomato halves cut sides down. Add the bacon rashers and cook until quite crisp on each side. Add the bacon to the plate and keep warm.
6. Cook the black pudding, if using, till browned on both sides. Remove and add to the plate. Check that your sausage is done.
7. Turn the tomatoes. Now slice the mushrooms and add them to cook gently, turning once or twice. Add the tomatoes and mushrooms to the plate.
8. Add a bit more oil. Crack the egg and let it slip gently out on to the pan. Use a spatula to flick oil over the yolk to help it cook. Or if you like it cooked on both sides then use a fish slice to turn the whole thing over. Give side two another half minute. Serve everything together.

For 1
Ingredients

3 tomatoes or as many
  as takes your fancy
1 garlic clove, chopped
Fresh basil or a little
  thyme or oregano
Salt and black pepper
Olive oil
2 slices ciabatta or other
  open-textured bread

Tomato bruschetta

Just about my favourite breakfast. This works with any full-flavoured tomato. Variety of bread is key here. Ciabatta picks up all those great flavours. Griddle till it's marked for authentic effect. This makes for a really healthy start to the day. Tomatoes are packed with good things that protect the body from disease and olive oil is one fat that is actually good for you. Rub a garlic clove over the bread if you don't want to add it to your tomatoes. If you want to believe you're on holiday, put on the shades.

Method

1. Preheat grill or griddle.
2. Chop your tomatoes roughly and put in bowl.
3. Add chopped garlic, plenty of basil, seasoning, and a drizzle of oil.
4. Griddle or grill sliced bread.
5. Drizzle oil on toast.
6. Pile tomato mix on toast. Eat immediately.

French omelette

I don't know why people make a fuss about omelettes. They're really easy to make. And once you're down with the basic technique you can do loads with them. This is a dish that's fast enough to stick together on a busy weekday. But I like to make it in the holidays or at weekends. Then I can take time to decide what I'm going to put in it.

Method

1. Break the eggs into a bowl. Add the water, salt and pepper. Use a fork to whisk the eggs with the water and seasonings.

2. Heat a frying pan or omelette pan. The hotter the pan, the better the omelette. Add the oil or butter – it will sizzle.

3. Add the egg mixture immediately and stir a couple of times. Work quickly.

4. Hold the pan in one hand and your fork in the other. Use the fork to pull the edges of the omelette towards the centre. Tip the pan so the runny stuff takes its place at the edge. Repeat three or four times.

5. When it's almost set sprinkle your chosen filling over the top.

6. Stick a spatula under one side and fold one half over the other. Plate. Serve. Eat.

For 1
Ingredients

2 eggs
2 teaspoons water
Salt and black pepper
2 teaspoons olive oil or 25 g/1 oz butter

Eat with:

SWEET: Runny honey or a little warmed jam.

SAVOURY: Cheese, cooked ham, bacon, fresh herbs, mushrooms, or tomato.

VARIATION
Fry diced onion, then bacon and mushroom or savoury favourites. Cook together till soft. Add the egg and cook through. Serve flat.

Cool, quick lunches...

Lunch? Don't skip it. It keeps you going. Eat it at any time between eleven and three. Often the best lunch happens when you get lots of bits together and put them on the table. Stuff left over from last night or the weekend. A bowl of **brilliant chicken soup** maybe to team up with a fantastically inventive **sandwich**. Something snacky to eat with **cheese**. Some great **fruit** or a tasty **salad**.

Make lunch the top time of the day at school. Power yourself through until you get home. What's in your pack-up can cheer you up and rev you up. Take in a flask of **soup**. Chuck some **salads** in a box. Make school eats as interesting as home ones or you'll end up chucking them away and heading for the chip shop.

For 1
Ingredients

1 small skinless chicken breast
Olive oil
Squeeze of lemon juice
Chopped fresh herbs of your choice, e.g. parsley, tarragon, coriander
2 slices pancetta or 2 rashers good bacon
1 chunk ciabatta or 2 slices good white bread
1 garlic clove, cut in half
Mayonnaise
Mango chutney
Tomato slices
Salad leaves – lettuce, spinach or rocket
Salt and black pepper

Sandwiches

Ban boredom. Make great sandwiches. There are two rules.

1. Whichever bread you choose (white, brown, treacle, wholemeal, granary, rye, focaccia, ciabatta, tortilla wrap) check that it's really fresh.

2. Be inventive with fillings. Sometimes surprising flavours work brilliantly together.

Big sandwich griddled chicken, bacon and salad (with mayo & mango chutney)

Have one of these at home and you'll really enjoy yourself. Put one in your pack-up and you'll be laughing. Use best chicken breast. But even a bland bird gets the star treatment if you griddle and team it up with all these great flavours.

Method

1. Sling the chicken between two bits of cling film. Bash with a rolling pin to flatten and thin it a bit. Discard cling film. Brush the bird with olive oil.

2. Cook it. Get the griddle really hot. Sling the chicken on to sizzle. Cook for 2 minutes until brown. Turn with a spatula. Cook for another 2 minutes. Spike the bird with a knife to check it's cooked and looks white all through. Award extra time if it's a bit pink.

3. Finish it. Squeeze lemon juice over the bird in the pan. Spinkle with salt and any fresh herbs. Put it to rest on a plate
4. Get the pancetta or bacon in there. Sizzle till crisp. Remove.
5. Cut the ciabatta down the middle. Toast it cut side down on the griddle, or toast the bread slices.
6. Rub the garlic clove on the toasted side of the bread. Spread with mayo and mango chutney. Stick in the bacon, chicken, tomato and salad.

VARIATION
⭐ Slap in pesto, guacamole or garlic mayo to spread.

⭐ Chuck out the chicken and bacon – use avocado and cheese.

For 1
Ingredients

1 teaspoon white wine
  vinegar
Pinch of caster sugar
Chopped fresh dill
  (optional)
10 cm/4 in piece of
  cucumber, peeled
2 eggs
Dollop of mayonnaise
Wrap bread of choice
Salt and black pepper

VARIATION

Also delicious with:
chopped tomato;
gran's favourite cress;
a little curry powder,
mango chutney
and spring onion.

Egg mayonnaise & sweet & sour cucumber wrap

Egg mayo and cucumber make a great combo. But you knew that. Try dunking the cucumber in a sweet & sour dressing. It brings out the sweetness in the egg. The celebrity makeover makes all the difference.

Method

1. Make a marinade for the cucumber. Put the wine vinegar, sugar and dill (if using) into a shallow bowl.
2. Slice the cucumber thinly. Stick in the bowl of marinade.
3. Hard boil the eggs. Lower them into a saucepan of boiling water. Bring back to the boil. Time for another 10 minutes. Drain under cold running water, cracking shells.
4. Shell eggs. Mash in small bowl with mayo and seasoning.
5. Fill wrap or bread with drained cucumber and egg mayo.

Griddled courgette & cream cheese

Take this to school. Hold back – try not to eat it on the bus. Courgettes are amazing when you griddle them. Enjoy their slightly smoky flavour in this wacky sarnie.

Method

1. Preheat the griddle pan to hot.
2. Slice the courgette thinly lengthways. Brush one side of each slice with a little oil.
3. Lay the courgette slices oiled sides down on the griddle. Cook for 2 minutes on each side or until done.
4. Squeeze lemon or lime juice over the criss-cross browned courgette. Sprinkle with salt.
5. Spread cream cheese on bread. Layer on courgettes. Add torn herbs if using. Top sandwich or leave open. Delicious.

For 1
Ingredients

1 large courgette
Olive oil
Lemon or lime juice
Cream cheese – low-fat, plain or with garlic and herbs
1 piece French bread or ciabatta
Parsley or coriander leaves (optional)
Sea salt

VARIATION
Enjoy slatherings of hummus instead of cream cheese.

WHY NOT?
Make a great salad with a load of courgettes. Cook as above. Drizzle with olive oil. Toss them with herbs and a bit of chopped chilli if you go for heat, plus lemon or lime juice and sea salt. Stack on a plate for home eating or throw in a box for a tasty pack-up.

For 1
Ingredients

1 small skinless chicken
  breast, cut into bite-
  size pieces
1 pitta bread

COATING
Lemon juice
1 garlic clove, chopped
Good pinch of ground
  cumin
Good pinch of turmeric
Fresh coriander leaves,
  chopped (optional)
Salt

FILLING
1 tablespoon natural
  yogurt
1 tablespoon hummus
  (page 78)
Mango chutney
Cucumber, diced
Tomato, diced
Salad leaves, torn up

VARIATION
Skip the chicken. Fry
cubes of cold cooked
potatoes in a little oil
with chopped onion,
garlic, coriander,
cumin, turmeric,
salt and lemon juice.
When cooked, enjoy
with the hummus
filling and salad.

Spiced chicken in pitta with hummus

I really like the mix of cool and spicy flavours in this great combo. And it's a great way to eat "al fresco" – outside. The pitta pocket stops you spilling this all down your shirt.

Method

1. Coating: mix the ingredients in a bowl. Add the chicken pieces and toss them.

2. Heat the griddle. Use tongs to drop the chicken to sizzle on the pan. Turn and turn again till cooked through. Spike with a

knife to check for doneness (white all through). Remove now or the chicken will overcook and get leathery.

3. Preheat the grill on medium.

4. Filling: mix the yogurt and hummus.

5. Pitta: warm under the grill for a minute till soft and puffed.

6. Cut the pitta open lengthways. Slather with mango chutney and hummus. Stuff with chopped salad and spicy chicken.

Vegemite-lettuce

Don't laugh. This one tastes great and just happens to be one of my favourites.

Method Stick everything together.

For 1
Ingredients

2 thin slices white bread
Butter
Vegemite or Marmite
2 lettuce leaves

Tuna lemon mayo

Feel virtuous. The fish in this may well boost your memory. Or forget it and enjoy these classic flavours.

For 1

Ingredients

Small can tuna
Lemon juice
Black pepper
Mayonnaise
2 slices good bread

VARIATION
Add chopped cucumber, finely chopped anchovies, finely sliced spring onion or chopped gherkin.

Method

1. Drain the tuna. Throw it in a bowl.
2. Add a good squeeze of lemon, a good dollop of mayo and pepper. Mix with a fork. Taste and adjust flavours.
3. Eat between slices of good bread.

Try to buy dolphin friendly tuna.

Ham & Swiss cheese

Simple but satisfying. Have one of these when you're in the mood for totally plain eating. No salad or mayo. Won't leak on your books. Get your cheese and ham from the deli if you can.

For 1

Ingredients

Chunk of fresh baguette
Butter
Mustard (optional)
1 slice ham
1 slice Swiss cheese – or cheese of your choice

Method

Slice the baguette through in half and spread very thinly with butter. Layer with ham and cheese.

Prawn cocktail

Work a bit of magic on your mayo. This is the marie-rose sauce for traditional prawn cocktail.

For 1

Ingredients

2 tablespoons mayo
1 teaspoon tomato ketchup
1 clove garlic (optional)
Lemon juice
Black pepper
Handful peeled cooked prawns
2 slices bread

Method

1. Mix the mayo, ketchup, crushed garlic (if using), and a good squeeze of lemon. Taste and add a little pepper with more lemon juice if you like.
2. Stir in the prawns. Make a sandwich – open or closed.

Soup

QUESTION What's usually hot but is always cool?

ANSWER Soup.

You can use just about anything to make soup. Trainers, skateboards… No, seriously. Check out ingredients that you think will work. Sweat everything down in a bit of butter or oil. Grab yourself the right stock. Throw in fresh herbs. You'll have a great bowl of lunch in front of you pretty damned quickly.

Carrot soup with coconut & coriander

This great Thai-style soup is so sweet that you could almost believe that it's not healthy. But it's full of great body boosters and improves night vision. You've got to admit that could be useful!

Method

1. Peel and chop the potatoes and carrots. Chop the onion.

2. Melt the butter in a heavy bottomed saucepan. Tip in the onion with a pinch of salt. Cook gently on a low heat for about 5 minutes to soften without browning.

3. Add carrots and potatoes. Stir. Cover and leave to sweat for 10 minutes.

4. Add chopped coriander, stock or water, coconut milk, orange juice, a squeeze of lime, salt and pepper.

5. Boil, reduce heat, cover and simmer till the carrots are soft. This could take 30–40 minutes depending on the carrots.

6. Liquidize in a blender till smooth. Reheat gently, stirring, and check seasoning. Serve with the lime wedges for squeezing.

For 4
Ingredients

225 g/8 oz potatoes
675 g/1½ lb carrots
1 onion
50 g/2 oz butter
Bunch of fresh coriander
  leaves, chopped
900 ml/1½ pints
  vegetable stock or
  water; or 700 ml/28 fl
  oz water plus 200 ml/
  7 fl oz chicken stock
100 ml/4 fl oz coconut
  milk
Juice of 1 orange
2 limes, cut into wedges
Salt and black pepper

For 4

Ingredients

350 g/12 oz potatoes
1 onion
3–4 large leeks
50 g/2 oz butter
1 tablespoon chopped
   fresh sage or tarragon
   (optional)
900 ml/1½ pints water,
   vegetable stock, or
   chicken stock and
   water
Lemon juice
250 ml/8 fl oz milk
Salt and black pepper

Eat with: Grated cheese
(Cheddar or Gruyere), or
crumbled crisply grilled
bacon scattered on top.

WHY NOT?

Make chicken stock
from my Roast
chicken (page 153).

Delicious leek & potato soup

Get your daily portion of veg down in one. Leeks make a great smooth soup – perfect for putting in a flask. This one's buttery and savoury. Top tip: leeks can be grit monsters, so don't be coy. Give them a good wash, or you'll be finding field in your spoon.

Method

1. Peel potatoes and chop small.
2. Cut the green tops and root ends off leeks. Pull off the tough outer layers. Wash each leek, then cut along the length. Search out any grit. Rinse in cold running water. Drain and chop small.
3. Peel and chop the onion.
4. Melt the butter in a large heavy-bottomed saucepan.
5. Add the veg and herbs. Season. Stir with a wooden spoon to coat with butter. Cover the pan with a lid over a low heat and leave the veg to sweat for 10 minutes without colouring.
6. Add the water or stock and a good squeeze of lemon. Replace the lid and simmer for another 20–30 minutes until everything is soft but still fully flavoured.
7. Liquidize. Add the milk and reheat. Taste and adjust seasoning.

Brilliant chicken soup

I've inherited this soup. My dad's mum made it. My mum does. And now I do my own version. This is Mum's. She says it boosts the immune system. I say make it. It tastes cool.

Method

1. Peel and chop all the veg into bite sized pieces. Finely chop the herbs and onion.

2. Melt a dollop of butter with a slug of oil in a large heavy bottomed saucepan. Slap in the onion and celery with a pinch of salt. Cook gently without colouring till soft and see-through.

3. Add the crushed garlic, herbs and remaining veg. Stir till coated. Put the lid on the pan and let them sweat for 10 minutes.

4. Add stock. Raise the heat to boil, then simmer gently for 15 minutes.

5. Add pasta. Cook for a further 15 minutes or till veg are soft.

6. Add extra herbs, a good squeeze or two of lemon, and taste to check seasoning.

For 4
Ingredients

1.5 litres/2½ pints home made chicken stock (page 153)

1 large onion

1 leek

2 potatoes

3 carrots

1 celery stick

Few sprigs of fresh herbs (parsley, tarragon, sage or rosemary)

Knob of butter

Sunflower or vegetable oil

2 garlic cloves, crushed

Handful pasta – e.g. macaroni, broken spaghetti, farfalle, penne or other small shapes

Lemon juice

Salt and black pepper

VARIATION

At STEP 3 add finely chopped bacon. At STEP 4 add a 450 g/ 15 oz can chopped tomatoes, a squeeze of tomato puree and pinch of sugar. Serve with freshly grated Parmesan cheese and garlic bread. You've just made Italian Minestrone soup.

For 4

Ingredients

3 shallots
2 garlic cloves
50 g/2 oz butter
Sunflower or vegetable
  oil
350 g/12 oz field or flat
  cap mushrooms
1 rosemary sprig,
  chopped
2 slices white bread –
  crusts removed and
  broken into bits
1.5 litres/2½ pints
  chicken or vegetable
  stock or water
Grated nutmeg
Salt and black pepper
150 ml/¼ pint milk

Eat with: Toast fingers or
a giant cheese straw.

The best mushroom soup with rosemary & garlic

Did you know that herbs work like medicines? Rosemary makes food easier to digest. Garlic thins the blood and keeps vampires away. Eat this soup. Breathe on a teacher.

Method

1. Chop the shallots and garlic.
2. Melt butter with a slug of oil in a large saucepan. Throw in shallots and garlic. Add a bit of salt. Cook gently for 2–3 minutes, till soft but not coloured.
3. Peel mushrooms. Chop roughly. Chuck into pan and stir well. Add rosemary. Cover and cook gently for 10 minutes.
4. Throw bread into the pan. Add stock and a few gratings of nutmeg. Bring to the boil. Reduce heat. Cover and simmer gently for 10 minutes. Everything looks disgusting at this stage. Keep the faith – it'll be OK. Season.
5. Blitz soup in a blender till smooth. Add milk. Re-heat gently.

My fast Chinese-style chicken soup

I'm addicted to Chinese food. So I like to take a basic chicken stock and make it a bit oriental. This is my own pot noodle. Eat it with a Chinese spoon. (Chopsticks for the great veg and slippery noodles.)

Method

1. Peel and slice the garlic and ginger. Slice the spring onions.
2. Pour the chicken stock into a large saucepan and heat till simmering. Add the garlic and ginger with the soy sauce. Cover and simmer gently for at least 30 minutes.
3. Two-thirds fill a second pan with water and bring to the boil. Add noodles. Bring back to the boil, reduce the heat and cook for 4 minutes. Drain. Rinse in cold water.
4. When the stock is done, add the rice wine, fish sauce, spring onions and pak choi or spinach. Simmer for 2 minutes, till wilted.
5. Add the cooked noodles, coriander and lemon or lime juice to taste, with more soy, if you think it needs it.

For 1–2
Ingredients

600 ml/1 pint home made chicken stock (page 153)
6 garlic cloves, chopped
1 small piece fresh root ginger, chopped
3 spring onions
1 tablespoon soy sauce
1 tablespoon rice wine
1 tablespoon Thai fish sauce
100 g/4 oz dried egg noodles
Few leaves of pak choi or spinach
Handful fresh coriander leaves, chopped
Lemon or lime juice

VARIATION
Float slices of my char sui pork on the soup – turn your kitchen into a dim sum restaurant (page 97).

For 1
Ingredients

2 slices bread
25 g/1 oz butter
100 g/4 oz strong
  Cheddar cheese,
  grated
½ teaspoon English
  mustard
Worcestershire sauce or
  pinch of cayenne
  pepper
Black pepper
1 tablespoon milk or
  beer

WHY NOT?

Cream ingredients
with a wooden spoon.
Store in fridge for up
to a week, ready for
grilling on your toast.

Snacks with cheese...

The ultimate fast food. My favourite. Perfect with bread and fruit.

Welsh rarebit

The number one cheese on toast. This is cooked, then grilled in a dish. But it only takes a minute. Eat it with a big dollop of home-made apple chutney or your favourite relish.

Method

1. Preheat grill to max. Toast bread on one side. Slap in a shallow ovenproof dish, toasted side down. Reduce grill setting to medium.
2. Melt butter in a saucepan over low heat. Toss in cheese. Stir with a wooden spoon till it melts to smooth.
3. Take off the heat. Working quickly, add in mustard, shake of Worcestershire sauce or cayenne, and black pepper. Stir. Add beer or milk. Stir.
4. Spread the mix on the bread.
5. Stick under the grill. As the cheese melts and browns, it puddles up round the toasted bread.

Croque-monsieur

You'll find this top ham 'n' cheese snack on every cafe menu in Paris. To make croque-madame shove an egg on top and whack up your protein.

Method

1. Preheat the grill to medium. Butter both slices of bread. Spread one with mustard if using. Then ham, cheese, then ham again. Add the other slice of bread, buttered side down. Press together.

2. Slap under the grill. Turn half way through toasting. This is done when cheese starts to melt and ooze out.

3. For croque-madame fry an egg in a little olive oil and sit it on top of the hot sandwich.

For 1
Ingredients

2 thin slices bread
Butter
Dijon mustard (optional)
1–2 slices Cheddar or
** Gruyere cheese**
2 thin slices cooked
** ham**

Eat with: Fruit.
Tomato salad (page 155).
A sharply dressed green salad.

For 1
Ingredients

2–3 wedges of cheese
1 sharp eating apple
1 ripe tomato or a few
    cherry tomatoes
1 celery stick
Crisps
Apple chutney or other
    relish
Small piece of fruit cake
1–2 slices My mum's
    treacle bread (page
    152)
Butter

(page 152)

VARIATION
PLOUGHMAN'S LITE
If you need to break a
chip shop habit, slap
this on your menu and
make up your combo
from:
Bread, oatcakes or
crispbread;
Crisp lettuce in a
mustard dressing;
Edam or cottage
cheese;
Celery and/or carrot;
Pineapple, apple,
pear, grapes, or see
what fruit's around.

Ploughman's lunch

The cheese is the
thing for this. It's got
to be good. You don't
need much. But
make sure it's got a
real taste. I like to
pick out the ones with
weird names – like
Cuddy's Cave and
Maisie's Kebbuck.

Method

Slice or chop your ingredients. Set the plate up. Enjoy.

Ingredients

Baking potatoes
Butter
Salt and black pepper

Eat with: Any
of these toppings:
⭐ tuna and garlic mayo
⭐ guacamole and
cheese
⭐ baked beans mixed
with slices of fried chorizo
sausage
⭐ cottage cheese with
fresh fruit, nuts and
raisins
⭐ Bolognese sauce
⭐ ratatouille
⭐ coleslaw

Stuffed baked potatoes

First bake your potato. Then stuff it. Cook more of these than you need. Fridge them or freeze them. (They're brilliant for parties.)

Method

1. Preheat the oven to 200°C/400°F/gas 6.
2. Scrub or wash the potatoes well. Prick three or four times with a fork. Stick them into the oven for 1 hour.
3. When cool enough to handle slice each potato in half. Spoon the potato flesh into a bowl. Add butter, salt and pepper. Mash really well with a fork. Pile mix back into the skins and place on baking tray. Bake for 10–15 minutes.

VARIATION
At STEP 3 add any
of the following:
grated cheese;
a spoonful of pesto;
some chopped herbs,
Dijon mustard and
squeeze of lemon juice.

WHY NOT?

Bake a sweet potato in
the oven for 30
minutes. Slash it open
and eat plain or with
salt and butter.
Tastes fantastic.

For 2–4
Ingredients

200 g/7 oz feta cheese
2–3 tablespoons olive oil
2–3 fresh oregano,
parsley or thyme
sprigs, chopped, plus
a few whole sprigs
4 large ripe tomatoes
½–1 cucumber
½–1 red onion or 3 shallots
10 black olives
Lemon juice

VARIATION
HALLOUMI SALAD
Cut slices of halloumi
cheese and brush with
a little olive oil. Slap the
slices on a hot griddle
pan. Cook till browned.
Turn with a spatula and
cook the second side.
Pile on top of the salad
instead of feta. Drizzle
with oil and lemon or
lime as STEP 3. Add a
little finely chopped
chilli if you like heat.

For 2
Ingredients

175 g/6 oz penne
3 tablespoons French
dressing (page 150)
2 spring onions, sliced
½–1 cucumber, diced

Salads…

Can be as simple as a bowl of crisp lettuce with a great home-made dressing. Or something else…

Greek salad

I love this – cubes of salty feta cheese marinated in oil and herbs, piled on a heap of black olives, ripe tomatoes and cool cucumber. All drizzled with fruity olive oil and a squeeze of lemon. You're either on a Greek island or you're at home watching the lunchtime episode of Neighbours. Enjoy this with a soft warm pitta bread.

Method

1. Cube the feta cheese. Stick it in a bowl. Drizzle half the oil and scatter half of your herbs over the top. Stir to coat.
2. Roughly chop tomatoes and cucumber. Slice the onion finely. Stick these in a serving bowl with the olives and fresh herbs.
3. Drizzle the remaining olive oil and a good squeeze of lemon juice over this bowl.
4. Top with the feta and more herbs.

Pasta salad

Pasta works brilliantly with a load of different tastes. So experiment. Throw in the things you like best. The thing is to let it soak up the salad dressing while it's cooling. That way it downloads maximum flavour.

Method

1. Boil a large saucepan of salted water. Add the pasta. Boil again and stir. Boil for 10–15 minutes or as packet instructions.

2. Drain pasta in a colander. Stick it in a bowl. Add 2 tablespoons of French dressing, mix well and leave to cool.
3. Add the spring onions, cucumber, tomato and herbs. Add seasoning to taste and stir well. Add remaining dressing and extra lemon juice to taste. Stir.

2 tomatoes, diced
Handful of chopped
  fresh parsley and basil,
  or coriander
Salt and black pepper

VARIATION
Add any of the following to pasta salad:

★ a can of drained tuna

★ cubes of mild cheese

★ hard-boiled egg with bits of crisp-fried pancetta or rindless bacon

VARIATION
At STEP 2 dunk the bread in pesto before baking.

Italian panzanella salad

This is a sharp little summer salad. The bread's the key. Don't use packet. Get ciabatta or a crunchy crusty job. It's great for soaking up all the punchy flavours.

For 4–6
Ingredients

- 1 ciabatta or small sized crusty loaf
- 2 tablespoons olive oil, plus extra for cooking
- A little fresh basil or parsley, to taste
- 4 large fat tomatoes, roughly chopped
- ½ fat cucumber, peeled and cubed
- 1 red onion, chopped
- 1 garlic clove, chopped
- 1 tablespoon red wine vinegar
- Pinch of sugar
- Sea salt and black pepper

Method

1. Preheat the oven to 200°C/400°F/gas 6.
2. Drizzle a little olive oil on a baking tray and sprinkle on a little sea salt. Cut the bread into rough chunks and tip on to the tray. Turn the chunks to coat them. Bake till golden (5–10 minutes).
3. Roughly chop the herbs. Chuck the tomatoes, cucumber, onion, garlic and herbs in a bowl. Add bread while still warm.
4. Drizzle over the oil, vinegar and season with sugar, salt and pepper. Stir gently to mix. Leave to stand for 10 minutes.

Tomato, avocado & mozzarella salad

Buffalo mozzarella is a cheese made from buffalo milk. Weird! But its creamy taste is perfect for this. Use the best you can find, not the stuff sold in blocks. That's only good for topping pizzas. Plate this up so the slices overlap. Finish with a great dressing.

Method

1. Make the dressing (page 150).
2. Slice round the middle of the avocado. Twist and pull it in two. Remove the stone. Peel off the skin.
3. Slice the tomatoes, cheese and avocado thinly.
4. Alternate overlapping slices of each ingredient on the plate.
5. Drizzle with dressing. Distribute leaves of basil.

For 2
Ingredients

My everyday French
  dressing (page 150)
1 large ripe avocado
2 large tomatoes
225 g/8 oz mozzarella
  cheese
Fresh basil leaves

Eat with: A slice of my Italian pizzabread.

For 4–6

Ingredients

375 g/13 oz packet puff
  pastry
3 tablespoons fresh
  pesto
5–6 vine-ripened
  tomatoes
Fresh basil or thyme
Sea salt and black
  pepper
Flour for rolling out
Olive oil for greasing
Egg for brushing

VARIATION

GARLIC MUSHROOM
Slice and fry button
mushrooms in a little
oil and butter. Lay
over the pastry base.
Scatter with chopped
garlic cloves and
fresh herbs. Bake.

CARAMELIZED ONION
Finely slice onions.
Cook slowly in a little
oil and butter with a
pinch of sugar in a
heavy pan until soft
and caramelized. Lay
over the pastry base.
Scatter with fresh
herbs. Bake.

Tomato tart

This makes for a cool quick tart. Save time by using bought in pastry.

Method

1. Preheat the oven to 200°C/400°F/gas 6. Grease a baking tray with a little olive oil.

2. Dust a pastry board with a little flour. Roll out the pastry into a rectangle about 35 x 28 cm/14 x 11 in. Cut two half inch wide strips off down the length of the pastry. Brush these lightly with milk then stick them, one each side, onto the main rectangle so that it's got a border on the two edges. Lay it out on your baking tray. Prick base lightly all over with a fork to stop it ballooning up.

3. Using a spatula, spread the pesto thinly over the pastry.

4. Thinly slice the tomatoes and lay them over the pesto.

5. Brush the pastry frame with beaten egg. Season with salt and pepper and scatter with whole basil leaves or chopped thyme.

6. Put in the oven to bake. Check after 20 minutes and leave longer if necessary. The bottom needs to be cooked and the edges browned and puffed up.

7. Remove from oven. Drizzle over a little oil and sprinkle with sea salt before serving.

School recovery

Hey, school's out for the day. And if you're anything like me you'll want to slump down on to the sofa for a bit and celebrate the occasion. **INGREDIENTS:** one cat (if she's in), a bit of TV to clear the brain (essential before homework) and something brilliant to eat or drink.

METHOD: Cruise the cake tin and fridge to see what's in. Hang around the kitchen putting it together. Avoid all questions like "So what did you do at school today?" Treat yourself to a slice of **lemon**

drizzle or **apple cake**. Or a **home-baked scone** with raspberry jam and cream. Make a batch of **biscuits**. If you've got the energy, a bit of light cooking is great therapy.

RESULT: eat, recover, re-charge, fantastic.

Ingredients

Makes 12

175 g/6 oz soft brown
  sugar
175 g/6 oz butter
1 generous tablespoon
  golden syrup
275 g/10 oz porridge
  oats
1 teaspoon ground
  ginger (optional)

WHY NOT?

Grab one of these if
you're late, for a
mobile breakfast.
They're a great shape,
and won't crack up in
pack-up or picnic.

VARIATION

At STEP 2 add finely
chopped dried apricots.
Or sprinkle in a handful
of desiccated coconut.

Flapjacks

Make better flapjacks than anyone else. Here's the secret. Leave the mix to sit for 15 minutes before you stick them in the oven. I don't know why but it makes all the difference. Great with a mug of tea and a music magazine.

Method

1. Grease a 20 cm/8 in square baking tin measuring about 4 cm/1½ in deep with a bit of extra butter.
2. Put the sugar, butter and syrup to melt in a large saucepan over a gentle heat. Stir with a wooden spoon.
3. Remove the pan from the heat. Tip the oats into the pan. Add the ginger (if using). Mix well.
4. Pour the mixture into your prepared tin. Use your hands or a spatula to level it off. Leave to stand for 15 minutes. Preheat the oven to 150°C/300°F/gas 2 while the mixture is standing.
5. Bake for at least 40 minutes, till golden and still a little soft in the middle. The mix will firm up as it cools.
6. Leave to cool in the tin. When the mixture has cooled slightly, cut it into squares. Take them out when cold and firm.

Apple cake

So you've got to rush out for the next class or a training session? Grab a slice of this great apple cake first. It's good and light and will power you through it.

Method

1. Preheat the oven to 180°C/350°F/gas 4.
2. Whack some butter round a 20 cm/8 in round deep cake tin with a loose base. Line the bottom and sides with greaseproof paper.
3. Peel, core and chop the apples into 5 mm chunks.
4. Beat the sugar and butter together in a large bowl. When soft and pale add the beaten eggs bit by bit, beating all the time.
5. Sift flour, baking powder and spices over the mix. Fold in using a large metal spoon with a big scooping movement to mix the cake and minimize air loss.
6. Gently fold in the apple, marmalade, orange or lemon rind, and essence. Add a little milk till the mix is soft enough to just drop off the spoon. Dollop into tin.
7. Bake for 1 hour. Test with a skewer or cocktail stick. It should come out clean. Remove when done. Sit on rack to cool. Sieve icing sugar over the top.

Ingredients

675 g/1½ lb cooking apples (about 3 apples)
75 g/3 oz softened butter
1 tablespoon lemon or orange marmalade
175 g/6 oz soft brown sugar
2 large eggs, beaten
225 g/8 oz plain flour
2 teaspoons baking powder
½ teaspoon ground mixed spice
½ teaspoon ground cinnamon
1–2 tablespoons milk
Grated rind of 1 lemon
3 drops natural almond essence (optional)
Dusting of icing sugar

WHY NOT?

Eat warm as a pudding with mascarpone, ice-cream, cream or custard.

Makes 16
Ingredients

- 200 g/7 oz butter, well softened
- 75 g/3 oz caster sugar, plus extra for rolling
- 150 g/5 oz plain flour
- 150 g/5 oz self-raising flour
- ½ teaspoon natural vanilla essence
- Pinch salt

VARIATION
Make one big shortbread biscuit. Spread with whipped cream. Pile it high with strawberries and raspberries.

Makes 12
Ingredients

- 225 g/8 oz plain flour
- 2 teaspoons baking powder
- 50 g/2 oz sugar
- Rind of 1 lemon
- 1 large egg
- 225 ml/8 fl oz milk
- 4 drops vanilla extract
- 50 g/2 oz melted butter
- 125 g/4 oz blueberries
- 25 g/1 oz dried apricots, finely chopped

Vanilla shortbread

I used to take these into school for fundraisers when I was a kid. We'd sandwich them with jam. Or ice them in bright colours. Sad thing is, I still really like them.

Method

1. Preheat oven to 150°C/300°F/gas 2. Grease two baking trays with a bit of extra butter. Line with baking paper (optional).
2. Cream really soft butter and sugar together with a wooden spoon. Beat until mixture is pale and soft.
3. Sift in the flours. Add vanilla essence. Beat everything together with the spoon, then finish off by using your hands to pull the dough together into a smooth soft ball.
4. Put the dough on a surface lightly dusted with flour and sugar. Roll out the dough to about 5 mm/¼ in thick. Cut out rounds or cool shapes with a cutter. Place on baking trays.
5. Bake for 30–35 minutes. Sprinkle with a little sugar. Leave on the tray to firm up, then store in an airtight tin.

Blueberry and apricot muffins

Chuck these together in the ad break – they're ready to eat by the end of your programme. Muffins fill the gap and make a great fruity snack. Re-heat leftovers for next day's breakfast.

Method

1. Preheat oven to 200°C/400°F/gas 6.
2. Sift flour and baking powder into large bowl. Add sugar and grate in lemon rind. Make a well in the centre of the mix.
3. Beat egg in a separate bowl then add the milk, vanilla extract, melted butter, blueberries and apricots.

4. Tip the fruity mix into the dry ingredients. Mix and stir well.
5. Put 12 muffin cases into a tin. Divide the mix equally between the cases.
6. Bake for 20 minutes or till done. (NB Home muffins don't rise like commercial ones but they'll taste great.)

Ingredients

Makes 10

225 g/8 oz self-raising flour
1 teaspoon baking powder
50 g/2 oz butter
25 g/1 oz caster sugar
About 150 ml/5 fl oz milk
Beaten egg, to brush
Granulated sugar, to sprinkle
Pinch salt

Eat with: Jam and whipped cream for an impressive cream tea. Make tea – in a pot.

VARIATION

SWEET
Add chopped dates, grated orange and lemon rind, sultanas and cinnamon at STEP 4.

SAVOURY
Leave out sugar. Add a pinch of dry mustard at STEP 2. Add 1 tablespoon grated Parmesan cheese, or cheese and chopped spring onion at STEP 3.

Scones

Claim them back! Scones aren't just for grannies. Make yourself up a batch and eat them as they are, with a bit of butter. The secret with scones is to keep everything light. Treat the dough with respect. Don't slap it round like a bread dough.

Method

1. Preheat oven to 220°C/425°C/gas 7. Grease a baking tray with a bit of extra butter.
2. Sift the flour, salt and baking powder high over and into a large bowl. Add the butter cut into small pieces.
3. Rub the flour and butter gently between your fingertips with your hands held high well over the bowl so that the mix drops back in. Repeat until there are no lumps of butter, but it doesn't have to be invisible, just fine. Stir in the sugar.
4. Add milk and mix lightly with a fork to make a soft but not sticky dough. Use your hands to bring the dough together.
5. Place on a well-floured board. Handle lightly. Roll it out gently – tease it, no pressure – to 2.5 cm/1 in thick.
6. Cut out 5 cm/2 in rounds with a floured cutter. Don't twist. Re-form dough. Repeat.
7. Place on baking tray. Brush with egg. Sprinkle with sugar. Bake for 12–15 minutes, or till risen, crunchy topped and golden. Cool on rack.

Chocolate satsumas

My brother Tom's favourites. They may sound a bit weird but they really work.

Method

1. Break the chocolate up into a heatproof bowl. Place over a saucepan of barely simmering water. The bowl base should be above the water. Stir once or twice as the chocolate melts.

2. Cover a couple of baking trays or boards with greaseproof paper. Peel the satsumas. Get as much white pith off as you can, but don't go crazy.

3. Dip each satsuma into the chocolate. Turn to coat. Using a large spoon helps. Lift each fruit out on to the trays. Fill in any gaps with spare melted choc. Leave to set somewhere cool.

Ingredients

250 g/9 oz good milk chocolate
4–6 satsumas

WHY NOT?

Drizzle melted white and then dark choc over top for posh.

Melt a large bar of milk chocolate over a pan of water. Pour in rice crispies. Stir to coat. Spoon into bun cases to set. Delicious.

Ingredients

175 g/6 oz butter, well softened

175 g/6 oz self-raising flour

175 g/6 oz caster sugar

1½ teaspoons baking powder

3 large eggs

1 teaspoon natural vanilla essence

Jam and whipped cream

VARIATION

FRUITY Use raspberries or strawberries to fill.

LEMONY At STEP 2 add grated rind of 1 lemon. At STEP 6 fill with lemon curd.

Light sponge cake with raspberry jam & cream

My grandad took a slice of this cake out to the fields in a tin every morning to keep him going. He did it for fifty years. Which makes how many cakes? We don't have it quite so often – but I like it just as much.

Method

1. Preheat oven to 180°C/350°F/gas 4. Grease two 20 cm/8 in sandwich tins with butter and line base with baking paper.

2. Sift the flour and baking powder into a large bowl. Add the eggs, butter, sugar and vanilla essence. Beat with a hand-held electric mixer or beat furiously with a wooden spoon. The mixture should be pale and creamy, and soft enough to drop easily off a spoon – add a splash of warm water if it doesn't.

3. Spoon the mix equally between the tins. Use a spatula to level it out.

4. Bake for 30 minutes. Don't open the oven door till then or they will sink. The cakes should be risen, golden and shrinking from the sides. Gently press the middles – they should be firm but springy.

5. Leave for a couple of minutes, then slip a knife around the sides of each cake to loosen. Put a rack over the top of the cake and turn it over, holding the tin and rack with an oven glove. Lift off the tin. Peel off the paper carefully. Repeat with other sponge. Leave to cool on rack.

6. Spread one cake with raspberry jam and whipped cream. Stick the other on top. Sift icing sugar over. Brilliant!

Lemon drizzle cake

I can eat half of this in one go. I really love the way the glaze sinks down into the cake leaving a slightly sugary lemon topping. A great cake for when you're lazing down on the sofa and chilling out.

Method

1. Preheat oven to 160°C/325°F/gas 3. Grease a 1 kg/2 lb loaf tin with butter. Line base with greaseproof paper and grease.

2. Whack the butter and sugar into a large bowl. Beat with a wooden spoon till creamy, pale and soft.

3. Beat the eggs lightly. Dribble them into the mix and keep beating. If the mix starts to curdle, beat in a bit of flour and just keep going. It'll still taste great.

4. Sift the flour over the mix and add the lemon rind. Fold this into the mix with a metal spoon using large, figure-of-eight scooping movements. Gently mix in the milk and lemon juice.

5. Spoon the mix into your tin, spread it and bake for 55–60 minutes without opening the door. Stick a skewer into the cake – when cooked, it will come out clean.

6. Prick cake all over. For the glaze, mix the lemon juice into the icing sugar. Pour over hot cake in the tin. Remove after 15 minutes. Cool on rack.

Ingredients

175 g/6 oz butter, softened

175 g/6 oz caster sugar

2 eggs

175 g/6 oz self-raising flour

Grated rind of 1 lemon

4 tablespoons milk

1 tablespoon lemon juice

GLAZE

Juice of 1 lemon

2–3 tablespoons icing sugar, sifted

Makes 14

Ingredients

100 g/4 oz self-raising
flour
1 teaspoon bicarbonate
of soda
2 teaspoons ground
ginger
Pinch of ground mixed
spice (optional)
PInch of ground
cinnamon (optional)
50 g/2 oz butter
40 g/1½ oz demerara
sugar
2 tablespoons golden
syrup

VARIATION
Use caster sugar
instead of demerara
sugar for softer
biscuits.

Polly's ginger biscuits

Nobody makes these better than my sister. They're
very gingery and totally delicious.

Method

1. Preheat the oven to 190°C/375°F/gas 5. Grease a couple of
large baking trays with a bit of extra butter.
2. Sift the flour, bicarbonate of soda, ginger, mixed spice and
cinnamon (if using) into a large mixing bowl.
3. Throw the butter into the bowl and rub it into the mixture
with your fingertips till it looks like very fine breadcrumbs. Stir in
the sugar.
4. Add the syrup. Use a fork to stir the mix together into a soft
biscuit dough. If too dry add a little more syrup.
5. Roll the mixture into about 14 small balls. Divide between
trays, leaving plenty of room between. They spread.
6. Flatten each biscuit very slightly using the bottom of a mug.
Bake for 15–20 minutes, till browned (watch they don't burn).
7. Cool biscuits on tray until they crisp up. Cool on rack. Store in
a tin when cold to keep them really crisp and crunchy. Don't
store with other biscuits – the flavour travels.

Banana bread

Grab a slice of this to eat when you're working on the PC. It doesn't crumble like standard cake. Spread it with a bit of butter or low-fat soft cheese and honey if that's to your taste. This is a brilliant way to use up over-ripe bananas.

Method

1. Preheat the oven to 180°C/350°F/gas 4. Use a bit of extra butter to grease a 1 kg/2 lb loaf tin. Line the bottom with greaseproof paper and grease it as well.

2. Mash the bananas till smooth. Lightly beat the egg and add to the mix. Add honey.

3. Drop the butter and sugar into another large bowl. Beat and cream furiously till pale and light.

4. Tip the banana mix into the creamed mixture. Beat in.

5. Sift the flour and salt. Tip a third of it into the mix. Stir it in then add a tablespoon of yogurt. Then add another third of flour and another spoonful of yogurt. Then the final third.

6. Pour the mix into the tin.

7. Bake for 50–60 minutes. Stick a skewer into the cake – when cooked it comes out clean. Remove from tin and cool on rack.

Ingredients

2 large ripe bananas
1 egg
1 tablespoon runny honey
50 g/2 oz softened butter
75 g/3 oz caster sugar
225 g/8 oz self-raising flour, sifted
3 tablespoons natural yogurt
Pinch salt

VARIATION
Throw in some chopped dates, walnuts, chocolate chips or finely chopped mixed peel.

Evening chill out

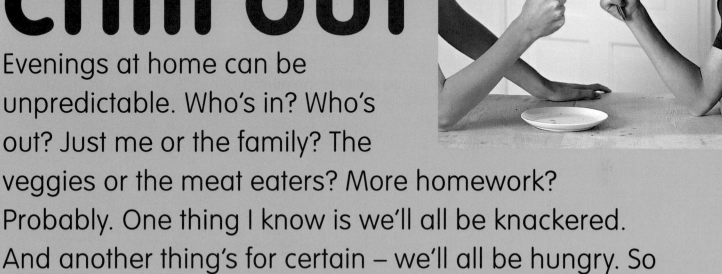

Evenings at home can be unpredictable. Who's in? Who's out? Just me or the family? The veggies or the meat eaters? More homework? Probably. One thing I know is we'll all be knackered. And another thing's for certain – we'll all be hungry. So what we need is no-fuss eating that's totally tasty but pretty straightforward. Any sort of ... **pasta** (faster and tastier than a defrosted pizza) ... **sausages** (good ones) ... **chicken** (not too heavy if you're out later) ... **spare ribs** ... **some veggie favourites**. Food to make us feel good ... get us sitting down at the table – chatting, eating, chilling and relaxing.

Ingredients

25 g/1 oz butter
2 tablespoons olive oil
1 large onion, finely
   chopped
3 garlic cloves, crushed
1 large carrot, finely
   chopped
1 celery stick, finely
   chopped
2 lb/900 g best-quality
   minced beef
2 x 400 g/14 oz cans
   chopped tomatoes
4 tablespoons tomato
   puree
Good pinch of sugar
Fresh thyme, oregano or
   basil, chopped
Freshly grated nutmeg
   (optional)
A little water or stock
Lemon juice
450 g/1lb spaghetti
Salt and black pepper

Eat with: Freshly grated
Parmesan cheese, garlic
bread and a dressed
crunchy green salad or
tomato salad.

WHY NOT?

Use the sauce to make
lasagne (page 115). Or
make cottage pie...
Slap sauce in dish. Top
with mashed spuds.
Bake as lasagne.

Spaghetti Bolognese

I haven't cracked how to eat it – but I can cook it. The sauce for this – a "ragu" – is rich, meaty with loads of tomato. The Italians let it simmer for 5 hours. This one's OK in 30 minutes but give it as long as you possibly can. Allow 125 g/4 oz pasta per person.

Method

1. Melt the butter in the oil in a large saucepan. Add the onion and garlic. Cook gently for 5 minutes, till soft and translucent. Add the carrot and celery. Cook for another 5 minutes.
2. Chuck in the mince and brown it up, stirring. Whack up the heat and throw in the tomatoes, tomato puree, sugar, herbs, nutmeg and salt and pepper. Stir. Add water or stock if too dry.
3. Reduce the heat, partially cover your pan and simmer the sauce for 30 minutes minimum.
4. Taste and adjust the seasoning, adding a squeeze of lemon juice, if you like.
5. Boil a large saucepan of salted water. Hold the spaghetti in the pan, lowering it as it softens. Boil for 12–15 minutes. Fork a piece out to check if it's tender. Drain in a colander.
6. Pile into bowls and slap the sauce on top.

Spaghetti Napoli (with tomato sauce)

This is all tomato. The first sauce I ever made. My brothers and sisters eat loads of this at uni.

Method

1. Heat oil in a saucepan. Add onion or shallots with a pinch of salt and cook gently for about 5 mins, till soft. Add garlic.

2. Tip in tomatoes, herbs, sugar, tomato puree, seasoning, torn basil and lemon juice.

3. Stir. Leave to bubble for at least 10 minutes. Add a little water if it gets dry. Taste and adjust seasoning.

4. Pile on pasta. Serve with grated Parmesan or Cheddar

For 2
Ingredients

1 tablespoon olive oil
1 onion or 2 fat shallots, finely chopped
2 garlic cloves, crushed
400 g/14 oz can chopped tomatoes
Pinch of sugar
2 heaped teaspoons tomato puree
Basil leaves, torn and whole
Good squeeze lemon juice
Salt and black pepper
175–225 g/6–8 oz spaghetti or penne, freshly cooked

VARIATION
Stir in 1 tablespoon of pesto or mascarpone cheese for a herby or creamier sauce.

WHY NOT?
Make spaghetti Napoli fredo by chopping fresh tomatoes. Add finely chopped garlic, basil, olive oil and a bit of balsamic vinegar. Pile the mix on hot spaghetti. Odd but magnificent.

For 4
Ingredients

450 g/1 lb spaghetti
1 tablespoon olive oil
6 rashers streaky bacon
   or 110 g/4 oz pancetta,
   roughly chopped
1 garlic clove, crushed
4–5 large eggs, beaten
75 g/3 oz freshly grated
   Parmesan cheese
Salt and black pepper

Eat with: Tomato salad.

Spaghetti alla carbonara egg and bacon pasta

Egg and bacon fans will love this. The hot pasta cooks the eggs. This is really fast food. Pasta releases chilling hormones by the way ... so this makes perfect eating when you need relaxing.

Method

1. Cook the pasta in a large pan of boiling salted water.
2. Meanwhile heat oil over low heat in frying pan. Cook bacon or pancetta with garlic till the fat runs and it's crisp. Turn off the heat. Leave in pan.
3. Drain cooked pasta in a colander. Return to hot pasta pan. Stir in the bacon and frying oil. Cool for 30 seconds.
4. Sling in the eggs and a little salt. Stir well to coat pasta. Add half the Parmesan, or to taste. Stir well. Add pepper.
5. Serve on hot plates with the extra Parmesan for sprinkling. Delicious.

VARIATION
Slice and fry mushrooms and use instead of bacon.
Use linguine in place of spaghetti.
Add 2 teaspoons of Dijon mustard to egg mix.

Sweet sticky barbecue ribs

These sticky ribs taste totally brilliant. The sauce caramelizes and softens the meat. Get up as much of the sauce as you can from the pan. It's too good to waste. Enjoy eating these with your fingers.

Method

1. Preheat the oven to 200°C/400°F/gas 6.
2. Mix all the sauce ingredients in a jug or bowl.
3. Lay ribs on foil in a big roasting tin. Pour the sauce all over the ribs and turn them a couple of times to coat them evenly.
4. Roast the ribs for about 1 hour, turning occasionally, till well browned and sticky.
5. Leave in a warm place to rest for 10 minutes.

For 4
Ingredients
16–20 meaty pork spare ribs (depending on size of ribs and appetites)

BARBECUE SAUCE
4 tablespoons runny honey
2 tablespoons brown sugar
1 tablespoon Worcestershire sauce
3 tablespoons soy sauce
4 tablespoons tomato ketchup or 2 tablespoons tomato puree
4 tablespoons red wine vinegar or cider vinegar
2 garlic cloves, crushed
1 teaspoon grated fresh root ginger or ground ginger
2 teaspoons English mustard powder or made mustard
Juice of 1 small orange
Pinch of paprika
Shake of Tabasco sauce (optional)
Salt and black pepper

VARIATION
For extra fruity sauce, at STEP 1 boil 2 stoned apricots or plums in water. Mash when soft and add to the sauce.

For 4
Ingredients

SAUSAGES
8 best pork or pork and
apple sausages

ONION GRAVY
Knob of butter
2 large onions, thinly
sliced
2 garlic cloves, crushed
Pinch of sugar
1 tablespoon plain flour
600 ml/1 pint chicken
stock or vegetable stock
1 tablespoon chopped
fresh thyme or sage
(optional)
1 teaspoon
Worcestershire sauce
(optional)
1 teaspoon balsamic
vinegar (optional)

MASH
700 g/1½ lb old
potatoes, peeled and
quartered
100 ml/4 fl oz milk
2 teaspoons English
mustard
25 g/1 oz butter
Juice of half a lemon
Chopped dill or parsley

Eat with: Stir-fried
cabbage with garlic or
Chinese greens with
spring onions.

Best sausage & mash & onion gravy

This is a great combo.
Good free-range
sausages. Creamy
mash. Onion gravy.
No sit-ups.

Method (do it in this order)

Gravy
1. Melt butter in a heavy bottomed pan. Add thinly sliced
onions, salt, sugar and crushed garlic. Cook gently for 10
minutes till soft and sweet.
2. Add flour. Stir for 2 minutes with a wooden spoon.
3. Gradually stir in the stock. Add herbs, Worcestershire sauce,
balsamic vinegar, salt and pepper.
4. Cover and simmer for 30 minutes. Taste. Adjust seasoning.

Mash
1. Boil peeled potatoes in water till soft. Check with knife. Drain.
2. Put milk, mustard, butter and lemon juice into the warm
cooking pan with the spuds. Mash together till smooth.
3. Stir the mash. Add herbs. Adjust taste. Transfer to an ovenproof dish. Cover. Keep warm in the oven for up to 30 minutes.

Sausages
1. Grill, fry or bake in the oven at 200°C/400°F/gas 6 for 20
minutes or till crisp, brown and irresistible.
2. Spoon mash on plates. Top with sausages and gravy.

Glamorgan sausages

Take a break from the game – set up a production line. Someone mixing the sausages. Someone rolling them in breadcrumbs. Making crisp, cheesy, veggie sausages. Eat with apple chutney or dunk in ketchup.

Method

1. Blitz bread in processor to make crumbs.

2. Tip 175 g/6 oz crumbs into a large bowl with finely chopped leek, shallot, crushed garlic, herbs, grated cheese, lemon rind, juice and seasoning.

3. Beat eggs with mustard. Set aside 1 tablespoon for later. Add rest to bind leek mix into a stiff paste with a bit of milk. Roll into 8–10 sausages.

4. Dip each in saved egg mixed with a little milk. Roll to coat in breadcrumbs.

5. Preheat grill on medium heat. Brush sausages sparingly with 2–3 tablespoons melted butter or sunflower oil. Grill on foil covered rack. Turn every couple of minutes for at least 15 minutes or till cooked, crisp and even.

For 4

Ingredients

250 g/9 oz fine white breadcrumbs (about 1 medium loaf)

1 leek, white part only, finely chopped

1 small shallot, chopped

2 garlic cloves, crushed

1 tablespoon chopped fresh dill, coriander leaves or parsley

1 tablespoon chopped fresh thyme or chives (optional)

175 g/6 oz cheese, such as mature Cheddar and/or Gruyere, grated

Grated rind of ½ lemon (optional)

Squeeze of lemon juice

3 eggs

2 teaspoons English mustard powder

3 tablespoons milk

Salt and black pepper

Eat with:

⭐ TOMATO SALAD: See page 155.

⭐ COLESLAW: See page 155.

⭐ CELERY AND APPLE SALAD: Chop apple and celery. Coat in sharp dressing. Add dates, nuts, or raisins.

For 4
Ingredients

3 large potatoes

1 large sweet potato

2 tablespoons sunflower
 or groundnut oil

1 large or 2 medium
 onions, finely chopped

4 garlic cloves, crushed

2 tablespoons korma
 curry paste

400 g/14 oz can
 chickpeas

500 ml/18 fl oz water or
 vegetable stock

Juice of 1 lemon

200 ml/7 fl oz carton
 coconut cream

1 tablespoon mango
 chutney

1 tablespoon tomato
 puree

4 tablespoons chopped
 fresh coriander leaves

200 g/7 oz can chopped
 tomatoes

2 tablespoons ground
 almonds (optional)

Big handful of spinach
 leaves

Salt

Eat with: RAITA:
Finely chop a 10 cm/4 in
piece of cucumber. Mix
with 1 chopped spring
onion, 2 crushed garlic
cloves, 6 tablespoons
natural yogurt and
seasoning.

Chickpea, spinach and potato curry

Look forward to a big bowl of this whenever you're freezing your arse off playing football or hockey (or whatever sports girls play in winter). Calm potatoes and mealy chickpeas get together in a great cool sauce. There's enough here to chill you out for a couple of evenings.

Method

1. Peel both types of potato and cut into bite-size chunks.

2. Heat oil in a large heavy bottomed saucepan. Add the onions, garlic and a pinch of salt, and cook till transparent.

3. Stir in the curry paste. Cook for 2 minutes. Add the potatoes and chickpeas. Stir till coated. Cook for 1 minute.

4. Add water or stock, lemon juice, coconut cream, mango chutney, tomato puree, two thirds of the coriander, tomatoes and almonds (if using). Turn up heat to boil; stir occasionally.

5. Reduce heat. Cover. Simmer very gently for 45 minutes, at least. Stir in spinach and cook for 2–3 minutes, till wilted.

6. Taste and adjust by adding more curry paste, lemon juice or tomato puree, to taste. Throw rest of coriander on top. Eat with rice, nan, cucumber raita, poppadoms and chutney.

Cauliflower cheese

I love a big plate of this comfort food. But there are rules. The sauce has to be thick and creamy with punchy seasoning and a really strong-tasting Cheddar. Making a sauce is one of the basic skills in cooking. You want it smooth, so get the ingredients measured out pretty exactly.

Method

1. Preheat the oven to 230°C/450°F/gas 7.
2. Sort the cauli. Strip off the leaves and break it up into florets.
3. Bring a large pan of salted water to the boil. Add the cauli. Cover. Boil gently for 8–10 minutes. Drain.
4. Make the sauce. Melt the butter gently in a saucepan. Stir in the flour and stir for a few minutes until the mix bubbles. Don't let it brown. Use a wooden spoon.

5. Take off the heat. Add the milk very slowly. Use a balloon whisk and beat constantly so that the milk and flour mix come together smoothly without lumps.
6. Put the pan back on the heat. Continue to cook – stirring – until the sauce thickens.
7. Bubble for 2–3 minutes, stirring so it doesn't burn.
8. Add half grated cheese, mustard, seasoning and lemon juice. Return to the heat and stir or whisk for 1 minute.
9. Put the cauli into a dish. Pour the sauce over. Top with remaining grated cheese. Cook for 20–30 minutes. Or slap under the grill till bubbling. Delicious.

For 4
Ingredients

1 large cauliflower
50 g/2 oz butter
50 g/2 oz plain flour
600 ml/1 pint milk
175 g/6 oz mature Cheddar cheese, grated
1 teaspoon English mustard powder
Juice of ½ lemon
Salt and black pepper

Eat with:
BAKED TOMATOES:
Cut tomatoes in half, place in ovenproof dish and top with pesto. Bake in the oven with the cauli for 10 minutes.

VARIATION
BROCCOLI CHEESE
Use broccoli instead of cauliflower.

MACARONI CHEESE
Boil macaroni in salted water for 12 minutes. Drain. Mix into the sauce and bake in oven for 30 minutes.

For 4
Ingredients

4 skinless chicken
  breasts
2 tablespoons pesto
80 g/5 oz soft cheese
  with garlic and herbs
8 slices Parma ham
Olive oil
1 lemon, cut in wedges
Handful fresh basil
  leaves
Salt and black pepper

Eat with:
ROASTED CHERRY
TOMATOES:
Roast some cherry
tomatoes in the oven. Put
them in a roasting tin and
drizzle with olive oil. Chop
in some garlic and fresh
herbs and add to the
tomatoes with salt. Roast
for 10 minutes.

Mixed-up chicks
Method

1. Preheat the oven to 190°C/375°F/gas 5. Slice the chicken
breasts length ways almost through. Open out.

2. Spread the insides of two breasts with pesto, two with garlic
and herb cheese. Close them up.

3. Wrap a couple of slices of Parma ham roughly round the
outside of each one. Lay in the dish. Season.

4. Drizzle with a bit of olive oil and a squeeze of lemon. Add
lemon wedges. Scatter herbs over top. Bake for 30 minutes. Eat
hot, warm or cold. Slice up and share. Eat the lemon flesh.
Don't waste those juices. Mop them up with some good bread.

Garlic chicken

Cook this for yourself when everyone's out. Garlic bangs loads of flavour into your chicken.

Method

1. Preheat the oven to 190°C/375°F/gas 5. Lightly grease an ovenproof dish.

2. Soften the butter with a wooden spoon. Chop or crush garlic into the butter. Add the herbs, a good squeeze of lemon juice and a pinch of salt. Mix well.

3. Slash each breast diagonally three times with a sharp knife. Fill the cuts with garlic butter. Place in the dish.

4. Bake for 20 minutes, till cooked. The chicken should be white, with no sign of pink meat. Serve with lemon quarters.

For 4
Ingredients

4 skinless chicken breasts
75–100 g/3–4 oz softened butter
2 plump garlic cloves
Good handful chopped fresh herbs – mix what you've got
Lemon juice
Salt and black pepper
Lemon

Spanish potato omelette – tortilla

For 4
Ingredients
110 ml/4 fl oz olive oil
3 onions, thinly sliced
3 large potatoes, peeled
  and thinly sliced
8 eggs
Salt and black pepper

Eat with: Salad;
great cold, especially as
picnic food.

I first had a slice of this as part of a plate of tapas (snacks) when we were on holiday in Spain. It looks like a cake, but it's actually an onion and potato omelette. This may not sound great – but I tell you, it is. Eat it warm in cake-like slices. The flavours relax – and so will you when you've eaten it.

Method
1. Heat the oil in a deep, large (25 cm/10 in) heavy frying pan. Add the onions and cook for 5 minutes, till they begin to soften.
2. Add the potatoes. Leave to stew together gently for 20 minutes. Stir from time to time so they cook evenly.
3. Crack the eggs into a large bowl. Whisk with a fork. Add salt and pepper.
4. Remove the potato and onion mix with a slotted spoon. Put it onto a plate covered with kitchen paper to soak up excess oil.
5. Pour all the oil out of your pan.
6. Put the potatoes and onion into the egg mix.
7. Put 2 tablespoons oil back into the pan. Turn up the heat a little.
8. Put the potato and egg back into the pan. Lower the heat.
9. Cook till set. Give it a gentle shake every so often so it doesn't catch on the bottom.
10. When it looks nearly set, but still a bit soft in the middle, run a knife round the outside. Slip it under a medium grill to finish the top.

VARIATION
Slice a tortilla in half. Cover bottom with rocket, tomato slices and ham. Replace top and cut into wedges.

Salmon – no bones

OK, I'm fussy about fish. I know it's a great food that we're supposed to eat loads of (the omega 3s in it boost the brain and allegedly improve your grades), but the last thing I want to do in the evening is worry about swallowing bones. So this is my relaxing salmon. Flash bake it in the oven, then drizzle it with teriyaki dipping sauce. Eat with some crunchy mangetout, garlic and spring onions.

Method

1. Preheat oven to 200°C/400°F/gas 6.

2. Place the salmon on a baking tray.

3. Mix soy sauce, sherry or wine, vinegar and sugar. Set aside about half the sauce. Brush the rest over fish.

4. Put the salmon in the oven for 5-10 minutes, or till done.

5. Heat the vegetable and sesame oils in a wok. Add the mangetout, garlic and spring onions. Stir-fry for 4 minutes.

6. Put stir-fry on to plates. Put salmon pieces on top. Drizzle rest of sauce over fish.

For 4
Ingredients

4 portions salmon fillet, about 150 g/5 oz each

3 tablespoons soy sauce

3 tablespoons sherry or rice wine

2 tablespoons rice wine vinegar

2 teaspoons caster sugar

STIR-FRY

1 tablespoon vegetable oil

1 teaspoon sesame oil

225 g/8 oz mangetout

1 garlic clove, crushed

4 spring onions, sliced

Impress the girls...

Serve any of these up when the girls come round. They're a bit lighter. A bit posh. But that doesn't mean that lads can't eat them. And you can really enjoy yourself taking time to put them together. A lot of girls I know are veggie. That's why there's not a lot of meat here. So look in the other sections for meaty ideas. Here you've got loads to impress – **Italian pizzabread with bits & pieces** (doubles up to make brilliant pizzas); dips like **guacamole**, **hummus** and **tzatziki** with **pitta bread stars**; **gazpacho** (which is the coolest soup going – literally); and **roast veg on couscous**. A bit of **shiny fish** and **salad nicoise**. Maybe you'll pick up some ideas for Valentine's Day cooking…

Pitta star with hummus, tzatziki, guacamole & tomato salsa

This looks really cool. And it's great for mixing tastes … dipping … eating… Thread a couple of warmed pittas together. Stand upright on plates to make stars. Spoon your dips round it … get chatting…

For 4
Ingredients
400 g/14 oz can
   chickpeas
2 garlic cloves, crushed
Juice of 1 lemon
1 tablespoon tahini
2 tablespoons olive oil
Salt
Paprika (optional)
Chopped fresh coriander
   leaves (optional)
Pine nuts (optional)

Hummus
Great served warm or cool.

Method
1. Drain chickpeas in a sieve over a bowl. Tip into food processor. Add garlic, lemon juice, tahini and a little salt.
2. Pour the olive oil and 2 tablespoons of water into a small saucepan. Heat but don't boil.
3. Add the liquid to the processor. Blitz till smooth. Add more water or lemon if the mix is too firm and blitz again. Taste.
4. Tip your hummus into a bowl.
5. Sprinkle with paprika, chopped coriander and/or a few pine nuts. Eat warm or drizzle with olive oil and chill.

For 4
Ingredients
2 garlic cloves, crushed
½ cucumber, peeled and
   finely chopped
300 ml/½ pint Greek-
   style yogurt

Tzatziki
This is cool … give it a bit of time to chill out.

Method
Mix the garlic and cucumber into the yogurt. Season. Cover and chill.

Guacamole

The best dip there is. Don't let this hang about too long. Avocado discolours when it hits oxygen.

For 4
Ingredients

- 2 ripe avocados (Hass are good)
- 1 garlic clove
- 2 shallots or 1 small onion, quartered
- Juice of 1 lemon or lime
- Cayenne pepper
- 1 tablespoon chopped fresh coriander leaves (optional)
- Salt and black pepper

VARIATION At STEP 3 add chilli for heat.

Method

1. Cut around each avocado. Twist the halves apart and ease out the stone with a knife. Scoop out the flesh using a teaspoon, right down to the skin to get the bright green colour.
2. Blitz the shallot and garlic in a processor or chop finely.
3. Add avocado, lime or lemon juice, a pinch of cayenne and salt. Blitz again. (Alternatively, mash the avocado and stir in the shallot or onion and garlic.) Blitz in the coriander, if using.
4. Tip the guacamole into a bowl, cover and chill briefly.

Salsa – this is hot...

For 4
Ingredients

- 4 ripe tomatoes
- 2 shallots or 1 small onion
- 1 fresh red or green chilli
- 2 tablespoons chopped fresh coriander leaves
- 1 lime
- Pinch of caster sugar
- Salt and black pepper

Method

1. Finely chop tomatoes and shallots or onion.
2. Slit chilli in half. Cut off stalk. Scrape out seeds. Finely chop the flesh.
3. Mix the chillies, tomatoes, shallots and coriander with a good squeeze or two of lime juice, sugar, salt and pepper.
Note: Don't touch your eyes or anywhere sensitive and wash your hands after handling chillies.

Ingredients

900 g/2 lb ripe tomatoes
1 red pepper, seeded
    and chopped
4 spring onions or 1
    small onion, chopped
½ cucumber, peeled and
    finely diced
3 garlic cloves, peeled
1 teaspoon fresh thyme
    or basil leaves to taste
3 tablespoons olive oil
1 tablespoon red wine
    vinegar or sherry
    vinegar
Pinch of sugar
250–350 ml/8–12 fl oz
    water to taste
Salt and pepper

GARNISH
½ red pepper, seeded
    and chopped
2 spring onions or ½ mild
    onion, chopped
A few black olives,
    chopped
Croutons
1 egg, hard-boiled and
    chopped
½ cucumber, peeled and
    finely diced

Gazpacho

This chilled red soup with loads of bits is great for sharing. There's no cooking involved – just slicing and dicing. It tastes as good as it is for you. Looks dramatic with little effort.

Method

1. Put the tomatoes into a heatproof bowl. Take care as you pour boiling water over them. Leave 2 mins. Remove them from the bowl with slotted spoon. Now you can peel their skins.
2. Cut tomatoes in half. Scoop and discard seeds. Chop flesh.
3. Put tomatoes, pepper, onion, cucumber, garlic cloves, salt and pepper, herbs, vinegar, sugar and oil into a liquidizer or food processor. Blitz till smooth. Add water.
4. Put the soup into bowl. Chill for 2 hours.
5. Arrange garnish on a big white plate. Sprinkle over soup.

WHY NOT?

Put a few ice cubes in each bowl if it's a hot day. People help themselves to garnish. Good with slices of pizzabread (page 82).

Ingredients

For 4–6

350 g/12 oz strong white bread flour

¾ teaspoon salt

1 sachet fast-action easy blend yeast

5 tablespoons olive oil

200–250 ml/7–8 fl oz warm water

Few sprigs chopped fresh rosemary

4–5 sundried tomatoes, roughly chopped

2 slices pancetta, Parma ham or chorizo, roughly chopped

8–10 black or green olives

2 teaspoons crushed sea salt

A few fresh rosemary or thyme sprigs for topping

Italian pizzabread with bits & pieces

This bread's got a lot going for it. A great look – sundried tomatoes, olives and herbs, and a fruity dough. Have it with deli stuff or something hot. Dip it into olive oil for eating and chatting. Re-think the topping to turn it into pizzas.

Method

1. Sift the flour into a big bowl. Add the salt and yeast. Use a wooden spoon to mix in 3 tablespoons of the olive oil, the water and chopped rosemary. Bring the dough together with your fingers. It should bind well and feel warm and sticky.

2. Throw the dough on to a floury surface. (Cheats – put the dough hook on your mixer and blast for 10 minutes.)

3. To knead by hand: Put on your music. Hang on to one side of the dough while you stretch the other away, bring it up and back around into a ball. Bash with the heel of your hand and thump with your knuckles. Bash it on to the board. Knead like this for 8–10 minutes, till the dough feels smooth and elastic.

4. Put your dough in a big bowl. Cover loosely with a plastic bag so the air is trapped inside. Leave in a warm place until doubled in size – an hour or two.

5. Brush a 30 cm/12 in pizza tin with oil. Turn the dough out on to a floured surface. Knead lightly for another minute. It will collapse. Lightly roll or stretch it into a circle to fit the pizza tin. Poke your thumb into the dough a few times to make it uneven.

6. Cover your bread with plastic again and leave for another 20–30 minutes, till risen.

VARIATION
PIZZABREAD PIZZAS
This dough packs loads of flavour on its own, so go easy on pizza toppings. At STEP 5 divide the dough into four and roll out into pizzas. Leave to rise on pizza trays.

Top with any of the following or your own combos. Drizzle lightly with olive oil. Bake as in STEP 9.

CLASSIC Tomato sauce (page 65), Parmesan cheese, Parma ham and basil.

MARGHERITA Tomato sauce, mozzarella and Parmesan cheeses, and basil.

SPICY CHORIZO Tomato sauce, pepperoni and Parmesan.

MUSHROOM Tomato sauce, mozzarella and Parmesan cheeses, garlic, mushrooms.

VEGETARIAN Tomato sauce, selection of roast Mediterranean veg.

ANCHOVY Tomato sauce, black olives, anchovies, basil and Parmesan cheese.

ROCKET AND PARMESAN CURLS Cook topped with made tomato sauce and Parmesan cheese. When cooked, scatter with rocket and more Parmesan curls, and drizzle with olive oil.

7. Preheat the oven to 220°C/425°F/gas 7.

8. Stick bits of sundried tomato, pancetta, ham or chorizo, olives and herb sprigs into the dough. Scatter with the sea salt. Brush or drizzle with the remaining olive oil.

9. Bake for 20 minutes, till well browned.

For 4
Ingredients

4 portions salmon fillet,
 about 150 g/5 oz each
2 garlic cloves, thinly
 sliced (optional)
4 shallots, thinly sliced
 (optional)
Fresh herb sprigs, such
 as dill, parsley and/or
 coriander
4 thin slices lemon
Bit of butter (optional)
Squeeze of lime or
 lemon juice
Salt and black pepper

ACCOMPANIMENTS
Sweet potato Fat chips
 (page 95)
Pesto
Mayonnaise
Tomato ketchup

Sexy salmon in foil parcels
sweet potato chips & pesto, mayo & ketchup to dunk

Shiny looks impressive. Package up your fish with lots of herbs and bits to create cool juices and infuse the salmon with flavour. Keep it nice and light. Share a big plate of healthy chips made with sweet potatoes.

Method

1. Preheat the oven to 200°C/400°F/gas 6.
2. Cut rectangular bits of foil big enough for each bit of fish plus generous extra.
3. Slap fish on the foil. Crowd it with bits of garlic and sliced onion, herbs and a thin slice of lemon. Squeeze a bit of lime or lemon juice. Season. Add a dab of butter (not essential).
Pull the foil up and scrunch to close.
4. Cook on baking tray for 15 minutes or till just cooked through.
5. Put an unopened parcel on each plate. Add a pile of chips. Spoon a dollop of each of the three sauces on each plate.

Roast veg on couscous with just-soft eggs

Sisters really go for this. So if you've got girls heading round – make extra, otherwise the kitchen's a battlefield. Roasting veg makes them ooze sugar.

Method

1. Preheat the oven 230°C/450°F/gas 8. Brush a baking tray with oil and lay the aubergines on it. Brush lightly with olive oil.

2. Chuck courgettes, peppers, onions and sweet potatoes into a roasting tin. Drizzle with oil. Add salt and rosemary – turn to coat. Chuck in the lemon. Put both tins in oven for 45 minutes.

3. Turn aubergines. Stir other veg and add garlic cloves and cherry tomatoes. Cook for another 10–20 minutes or till ready.

4. Put the couscous in a heatproof bowl. Season. Pour in the boiling water and cover with cling film. Leave for 4 minutes.

5. Add a bit of olive oil and a squeeze of lemon, and fork up to mix. Cover and leave for 2 minutes.

6. Boil eggs for 5 minutes, till softly set.

7. Mix the pesto and French dressing. Fork chopped parsley into couscous and tip onto plates. Pile veg on to couscous. Drizzle with the dressing. Top with shelled and halved eggs.

For 6
Ingredients

Olive oil
2 aubergines, cut into 5 mm/¼ in thick slices
3 courgettes, cut into chunks
2 red peppers, seeded and cut into thick strips
4 red onions, quartered
3 sweet potatoes, peeled and cut into chunks
Fresh rosemary sprigs
¼ lemon
8 cloves of garlic, peeled
12 cherry tomatoes
225 g/8 oz couscous
250 ml/8 fl oz boiling water
Lemon juice
6 eggs
4 tablespoons pesto
2 tablespoons French dressing (page 150)
4 tablespoons parsley

VARIATION

WINTER ROAST VEG: At STEP 2 peel and split 4 carrots, 2 parsnips. Peel and chunk 2 large sweet potatoes. Peel and quarter 3 red onions. Wash and dry 8 baby potatoes. Turn in oil and herbs with garlic cloves.
At STEP 6 poach eggs.

Salad Nicoise

For 4–6

Ingredients

350–450 g/12–16 oz
  fresh tuna steak
3 thick slices bread, cut
  into cubes
3 eggs
Salad dressing
  (page 150)
450 g/1 lb small new
  potatoes
Handful of fine green
  beans
3 rashers streaky bacon
  or slices pancetta
1 cos lettuce, roughly
  torn
4 tomatoes, roughly
  chopped
100 g/4 oz black olives
½ cucumber, diced
4 canned anchovy fillets
1 tablespoon capers
  (optional)
2 shallots, finely
  chopped
Mayonnaise
Salt and black pepper

MARINADE
Juice of ½ lemon
2–3 garlic cloves,
  crushed
2 tablespoons olive oil

Eat with: Bread or garlic
bread.

Tuna, salad, bacon, croutons and loads of other great tastes in a sharp dressing. Pile everything up on a big white plate and slap it in the middle of the table. Special!

Method

1. Slap fresh tuna in a dish with marinade ingredients.

2. Hard-boil eggs in a pan of boiling water for ten minutes. Cool under running water.

3. Make salad dressing. Whisk.

4. Boil potatoes for 10–15 mins till cooked. Drain. Sprinkle with 1 tablespoon of salad dressing while still warm.

5. Boil green beans for 4 minutes.

6. Cube the bread. Roll in a little oil on a baking tray. Bake for 10 minutes or till croutons are lightly browned.

7. Fry bacon or pancetta till crisp. Drain on kitchen paper. Crumble into pieces.

8. Tear up the lettuce. Roughly chop tomatoes and cucumber. Peel the eggs and slice in two.

9. Dry tuna on kitchen paper. Slap it onto a really hot griddle. Cook for 1–2 minutes till browned on the outside but a bit pink in the middle. Don't

overcook. It'll go leathery.

10. Put all salad ingredients onto plate or bowl. Pour dressing over. Mix in. Top with tuna, last few croutons, olives, shallots, anchovies and eggs (halved and topped with mayo).

VARIATION

CANNED TUNA SALAD
Skip the marinade and substitute two 200 g/7 oz cans of tuna at STEP 10.

CHICKEN AND PANCETTA SALAD
Use griddled chicken breast instead of tuna. Skip the anchovies, capers and potatoes. Top with curls of Parmesan cheese.

SALMON SALAD
Use salmon instead of tuna.

AVOCADO AND CHEESE
Skip anchovies, bacon, tuna and capers. Add dates, nuts, raisins, avocado and cheese.

Ingredients

- 2–4 duck breasts with skin (depending on appetite)
- 2 tablespoons honey
- 2 tablespoons soy sauce
- 1 tablespoon orange juice
- 1 teaspoon peeled and grated fresh root ginger or good pinch of ground ginger (optional)
- 2 packets Chinese pancakes

SAUCE
- 4 tablespoons hoisin sauce
- ¼ teaspoon sesame oil
- 1 teaspoon honey

GARNISH
- 1 cucumber, peeled, deseeded and cut into thin strips
- 8 spring onions, cut into thin strips

VARIATION
ORIENTAL DUCK SALAD
Lay the cooked duck on a salad of leaves, cucumber and onion. Add a handful of bean sprouts. Serve with oriental-style dressing (page 151).

Chinese-style duck breast with cucumber, spring onion & pancakes

You can go to the trouble of hanging a duck up on a coathanger overnight – then attacking it with a hairdryer to get that authentic Peking duck crisp skin. (We did. It sort of worked.) Or do it this way. See if those neat girls drop any.

Method

1. Preheat oven to 220°C/425°F/gas 7.
2. Mix honey, soy, orange juice, ginger to make basting sauce. Set 2 teaspoons aside.
3. Slash duck skin at diagonal 1 cm intervals.
4. Put duck on rack over roasting tin. Brush with basting sauce. Bake for 10 minutes. Baste again. Return to oven for 10 minutes.
5. Mix all sauce ingredients together. Put it into a bowl for dipping. Cut matchstick thin slices of peeled cucumber (ditch the seeds) and spring onions. Arrange them on a plate.
6. Test duck doneness. It should feel a bit springy and look a bit pink inside. Leave to relax somewhere warm for 5 minutes.
7. Cover pancakes in foil. Place on a small plate in a steamer or on a plate over pan of boiling water for 5 minutes.
8. Slice the meat thinly. Drizzle with a little reserved marinade.
9. Spread a pancake with a little sauce, add duck, cucumber and onion. Roll. Eat.

Herb gnocchi with sage and lemon sauce

Light. Lovely. Herby. Saucy. These work best with baked floury spuds. Girls (and lads) love gnocchi.

Method

1. Preheat the oven to 220°C/425°F/gas 7. Bake even sized spuds for 1 hour or till soft.

2. Scoop flesh into a bowl. Mash with a fork till really smooth. Add egg yolks, flour, salt and herbs. Knead briefly into a warm ball of elastic dough. Divide into four. Cover with a warm cloth.

3. Put one piece on a board. (Flour very lightly only if it gets sticky.) Roll into a long sausage as thick as your thumb. Cut this into 2 cm long pieces. Mark each lightly with a fork to make tiny grooves. Store side by side on a cloth. Repeat with rest of dough.

4. Bring a large pot of lightly salted water to boil. Turn down to simmer. Put batches of gnocchi in to cook very gently for 10 minutes. They swell a bit. Remove with a slotted spoon.

5. Make sauce: melt butter in a pan, add lemon, herbs and seasoning. Pour over gnocchi. Or toss with tomato sauce (page 65) or Bolognese sauce (page 64). Sprinkle with Parmesan.

For 4
Ingredients

800 g/1¾ lb floury potatoes (Maris Piper/King Edward)
2 egg yolks
100 g/4 oz strong plain flour
Pinch salt
1 tablespoon parsley or sage, finely chopped
1 tablespoon snipped chives

SAUCE
100 g/4 oz butter
Juice of a lemon
3 tablespoons chopped fresh sage or herb of choice
Sea salt
Freshly grated Parmesan

VARIATION
PLAIN GNOCCHI
Omit the herbs.

BUBBLING BAKED GNOCCHI
Mix cooked gnocchi with cooked tomato sauce (page 65). Place in a buttered ovenproof dish. Top with grated cheese. Brown in a very hot oven for 10 minutes or under a hot grill.

Mates round

Mates and parents at the same table can be well embarrassing. Your dad starts to tell bad jokes, your mum starts to fuss … so keep them apart. Or cook some great food as a major distraction.

Serve up some **mussels** steamed the French way. Or **French onion soup** with a **cheese crouton roof.** Try my mate Joe's **Thai green curry** with attitude. Chinese fans go for **char sui pork**. Just a couple of mates round? Make a **brilliant steak salad** and **potato rosti**.

If they can't be bothered to drag themselves away from the game? Dish up **pasta and meatballs in tomato sauce**. Or a great bowl of **chilli with cheese, sour cream, salsa and tortillas**. Snack on **chicken liver pate on toast**. Try not to drop the lot down the sofa.

Eating outside? Go for **home-style burgers** – beef or tuna – stacked with some great tasty stuff. Or have a **lamb kebab**. Be creative with salads, relishes and all the extras.

VARIATION
At STEP 5, ladle the soup into ovenproof bowls. Top each one with slices of toast till the surface is covered. Cover with grated cheese. Brown in a hot oven or under the grill till bubbling. HEALTH ALERT – hot to handle!!

French onion soup
with cheese croutons

Got a load of cold people round? Give them a big bowl of thick onion soup. Everyone who's been honoured by eating it loves it. Cook it up before you head out for the pitch. Warm it up when you get back in. Don't miss out on the rooftop crouton.

Method

1. Slice big onions into thin rings.
2. Melt the butter in a big heavy bottomed pan. Tip onions in. Add garlic. Stir to coat. Cover pan. Cook gently for 15 minutes.
3. Remove the lid. Add sugar. Cook onions gently for 40 minutes till soft and caramelized.
4. Increase heat. Add wine or cider. Bubble. Add stock. Season. Bring to the boil. Simmer for 20 minutes.
5. Toast bread slices. Top with grated cheese and grill till bubbling.
6. Ladle soup into bowls. Float the cheese islands on top.

For 4–6
Ingredients

4–5 large onions
3 tablespoons butter
2 garlic cloves, crushed
2 teaspoons sugar
300 ml/½ pint white wine or cider
1.8 litres/3 pints chicken or vegetable stock
6 slices baguette
100 g/4 oz Cheddar or Gruyere cheese, grated

Chicken liver pate

This makes a great snack on a bit of bread when you're hanging about watching someone else play a game. It's well creamy. It's got a cool taste. Eat on really loud bread. It might distract them.

Method

1. Roughly chop chicken livers. Cut and chuck away any white bits.

2. Melt dollop of butter in a frying pan. Cook shallots and garlic gently for 5 minutes without colouring.

3. Add bacon. Cook, turning, for 4 minutes.

4. Turn up heat slightly. Add chicken livers. Cook turning till browned on the outside but still a bit pink inside.

5. Now whack up the heat. Pour in juice or booze. Let it sizzle for a couple of minutes to finish cooking the liver.

6. Add herbs and season. Bacon's salty so go easy on salt.

7. Tip pate into processor. Add cheese plus a really good squeeze of lemon juice. Blitz till just smooth. Taste. Adjust seasoning. Add more cheese for smoother pate.

8. Spoon into a bowl. Cool for 5 minutes. Pour melted butter over to seal. Drop peppercorns and bay leaves on top for the look. Chill. Best after a day. Keeps for a week.

For 8
Ingredients

400 g/14 oz pack chicken livers
Dollop of butter, plus 2–3 tablespoons melted butter
3 fat shallots, finely chopped
3 garlic cloves, crushed
3 rashers back bacon
Thyme or herb of choice
175g /6 oz low-fat cream cheese
1 lemon
Big slug of sherry/ brandy or apple juice
Salt and black pepper

GARNISH
Peppercorns
1–2 bay leaves

Eat with:
Regular toast or melba toast.
MELBA TOAST
Toast packet sliced white bread. Remove crusts. Split each slice lengthways down the middle. Bake on a tray at 150°C/300°F/gas 2 till curled, browned and crisp (about 10 minutes). Delicious.

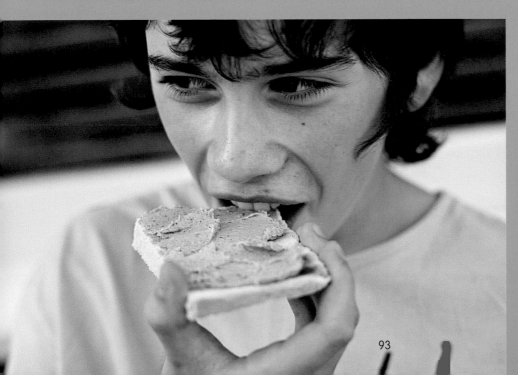

For 4
Ingredients

2 kg/4½ lb mussels
2 shallots or 1 small
  onion
3 garlic cloves, finely
  chopped
50 g/2 oz butter
Bunch of parsley
2 tablespoons double
  cream (optional)
300 ml/½ pint white
  wine or cider

Eat with:

Chilli sauce or garlic
mayo (see page 151).

Moules mariniere
mussels steamed in white wine & garlic

Mussels for me means moules mariniere. I love prepping and eating them. They're perfect for sharing with mates. You only need your fingers and a spoon. The liquor's brilliant so dunk in some bread. Do loads of fat chips to use up your mayo.

Method

1. Tip the mussels into a bowl of cold water in the sink. Remember: if they're cracked, float or won't close when tapped, chuck them out. <u>Never cook or eat them.</u>
2. Scrape or brush the shells clean. If they've got beards – black bits poking out from the shells – pull them out. Rinse.
3. Melt butter in a big pan. Cook garlic and onion for 2 minutes without browning.
4. Increase heat. Add wine. Boil up for 2 minutes.
5. Tip mussels into pan. Cover and cook over full heat for 2 minutes. Stir so the top and bottom mussels swap places. Cook for another 1–2 minutes, till the shells have opened.

6. Spoon mussels into bowls – a slotted spoon helps. Chuck any that are closed.

7. Add cream, if using, to the cooking liquor and heat gently – no boiling. Add parsley. Ladle into bowls, leaving any grit in the pan. Slurp from shells or use two half shells to eat mussels.

Fat chips

You don't want to be frying spuds when you've got mussels to cook. Bake these in the oven in a bit of olive oil. Great with chilli sauce and cool for parties.

Method

1. Preheat oven to 240°C/475°F/gas 9.
2. Scrub unpeeled spuds. Dry on kitchen paper. Chop each one into great big chip shapes.
3. Dry again. Put chips into a freezer bag with oil and salt. Shake.
4. Tip chips onto a baking tray. Bake for 30–40 minutes, till crisp and golden.

For 4
Ingredients
900 g/2 lb potatoes
2 tablespoons olive oil
Sea salt

VARIATION
Use sweet potatoes instead of spuds – peel them and use sunflower oil instead of olive oil. Bake till caramelized.

For 4–6
Ingredients

- 6 skinless chicken breasts, diced
- 2 tablespoons grapeseed or sunflower oil
- 4 shallots, finely sliced
- 1 stalk lemongrass, crushed and sliced
- 2 garlic cloves, crushed
- Grated rind and juice of of 1 lime
- 2 teaspoons ground coriander
- 2 teaspoons ground cumin
- 4 cm/1½ in piece fresh root ginger, grated
- 1 small green bird's eye chilli, seeded and thinly sliced
- 1 small red bird's eye chilli, seeded and thinly sliced
- 2 kaffir lime leaves
- 2 teaspoons Thai fish sauce
- 1 teaspoon peanut butter
- 400 ml/14 fl oz coconut milk
- Handful fresh coriander leaves, chopped
- Cashew nuts, chopped, to garnish (optional)

Eat with: Bowls of sticky Thai jasmine rice.

My mate Joe's Thai green curry

Joe cooks to his own style. He likes to take a bit of a basic recipe then chuck in extras to make up for stuff he hasn't got. This is his Thai green curry.

Method

1. Heat a large wok. Add the oil. Tip in the chicken. Stir-fry till sealed – changes colour – and almost cooked. Transfer chicken to a plate.

2. Add more oil if needed. Fry shallots, lemongrass and garlic till soft.

3. Add peanut butter, lime rind and juice, ground coriander, cumin, ginger, chillies, lime leaves and fish sauce. Cook for 2 minutes.

4. Add all coconut milk and most of the fresh coriander (save some for serving). Stir. Replace the chicken. Simmer for 30 minutes, stirring occasionally to stop the curry from sticking.

5. Tip into dish. Top with cashews and coriander.

Char sui pork

Me and my mates used to go to the all-you-can-eat Chinese in town. They've just closed down so maybe we ate too much. So now I cook this. Pork fillet's a really great meat for soaking up the sweet Chinese-style flavours.

Method

1. Mix marinade ingredients in dish. Add pork. Turn. Leave to marinade for as long as you've got.
2. Preheat oven to 200°C/400F/gas 6.
3. Lay foil over the base of a roasting tin. Put a wire rack on top. Put your fillet on rack. Roast for 20 minutes – brushing with marinade a couple of times.
4. Let pork relax somewhere warm for 10 minutes. Carve into thin slices.

For 4
Ingredients

2 x 450 g/1 lb pieces pork fillet

MARINADE:
2 tablespoons honey
2 tablespoons soy sauce
2 tablespoons hoisin sauce
1 teaspoon sesame oil
Pinch of Chinese five spice powder

Eat with: My stir-fry (page 98) and plain or egg-fried rice (page 146). Great with cooked noodles stir-fried with garlic, spring onion and beansprouts.

VARIATION
CHAR SUI TOFU .
Use 2 x 225 g/8 oz packs firm tofu instead of pork. Put on a chopping board and weight them down for 30 minutes to drain out water. Cut into cubes. Stick in marinade. Drain and fry gently in a little sunflower and sesame oil till browned all over. Tip marinade over. Top with slices of fried garlic and coriander. Enjoy with stir-fry.

For 2
Ingredients
- 5 cm/2 in piece fresh root ginger, peeled
- 2 garlic cloves
- 6 spring onions
- 75 g/3 oz green beans
- 75 g/3 oz sugarsnap peas
- 75 g/3 oz baby corn
- 75 g/3 oz broccoli
- 2 tablespoons sunflower oil
- 1 tablespoon sesame oil
- Pinch of sugar
- 1 teaspoon soy sauce
- Juice of 1 lime (optional)
- 2 tablespoons chopped fresh coriander leaves (optional)
- Cashew nuts (optional)
- Salt and black pepper

WHY NOT?
Cut whole oranges into boat-shaped segments, Chinese-restaurant style, for a fastfood pudding.

My stir-fry

This is just one veg combo. Sort the technique, then put together your own best ingredients. Use a wok or a big frying pan to stir-fry.

Method

1. Finely chop the garlic. Grate ginger. Trim, cut in half and slice spring onions lengthways. Cut beans, peas and corn into short diagonal lengths. Break broccoli into small bits.

2. Heat oils in a wok or large frying pan till hot. Add onion, garlic, ginger. Stir about for 1 minute.

3. Add other veg in turn – stirring between each.

4. Stir for another 5 minutes. Season with salt, pepper and sugar. Squeeze in lime juice, soy sauce, chopped coriander and cashews if using.

Chilli con carne

A classic. Give it a long, slow cook. Oven or hob. Go for gourmet – check out the toppings.

Method

1. Preheat oven to 180°C/350°F/gas 4 if baking. Heat half the oil in a large casserole. Tip in the steak (chopped small) or mince. Turn quickly till brown.

2. Lower heat. Add rest of oil, onion, garlic, chillies and coriander. Cook for a few minutes till soft.

3. Add beans, tomatoes, tomato puree, sugar, stock or water and cinnamon stick. Stir. Bring to boil.

4. Reduce heat. Cover. Simmer very gently or bake for 1 hour. Check and stir occasionally. Add a splash of water if needed.

5. Add the red pepper and stir. Cover and simmer it gently, or bake, for a further 40 minutes.

6. Taste. Season with salt and a squeeze of lime.

For 4
Ingredients

450–675 g/1–1½ lb chuck steak, chopped, or minced beef

2 tablespoons sunflower oil

1 large onion, chopped

3 garlic cloves, crushed

1–2 fresh green chillies, seeded and chopped

Bunch of fresh coriander leaves, chopped

400 g/14 oz can red kidney beans

400 g/14 oz can chopped tomatoes

2 tablespoons tomato puree

2 teaspooons soft brown sugar

175 m/6 fl oz chicken stock or water

1 cinnamon stick

1 red pepper, seeded and chopped

Lime juice

Salt and pepper

Eat with: Tortilla chips or tacos. Top with diced avocado, chopped fresh coriander, chopped red onion, squeeze of lime, grated cheese and soured cream.

For 4
Ingredients

4 x 150 g/5 oz fillet,
  sirloin or rump steaks
1 garlic clove, halved
Olive oil
100 ml/4 fl oz red wine,
  water or stock
Salt and black pepper

SALAD
Choose from:
  watercress, rocket,
  baby spinach, lettuce
2 shallots, thinly sliced
6 tomatoes, roughly
  chopped
Honey and mustard
  dressing (page 150)

VARIATION
TUNA STEAKS
Tender tuna makes a
great alternative. At
STEP 1 brush each tuna
steak with olive and
sesame oil. At STEP 3
griddle or pan fry for
2 minutes each side.
Add soy sauce,
lime/lemon juice.
Bubble. Turn tuna to
coat in the glaze.
Sprinkle with sesame
seeds. Sit on salad and
rosti. Enjoy with
Japanese ginger and
a slug of wasabi.

Steak salad & rosti

Perfect for when you've got just a couple of mates
round. Get one of them chopping salad. Another
doing rosti and dressing. You sit back and watch the
steak. (Working out when it's done takes a whole load
of focus.)

Method

1. Take the steaks from the fridge 1 hour before cooking. Rub
with garlic. Turn in a few drops of oil. Season with black pepper
– not salt – it toughens the meat.

2. Make the salad.

3. Get your griddle or frying pan really hot. Slap the steaks
down. Timing depends on heat of pan and meat and thickness
of steak, but as a guide:

RARE: 1–2 minutes per side and red inside.

MEDIUM RARE: 2–3 minutes per side and a bit pink.

WELL DONE: 3–4 minutes per side – browned through.

4. When cooked to your taste, sprinkle on salt and leave steak
to relax for 2–3 mins in a warm place. Leave whole or carve
into diagonal strips and lay over salad.

5. Chuck meat juices back into the pan to bubble up with a bit
of wine/water/stock. When reduced a bit drizzle over meat. Eat.

Rosti

Great as a support act. This looks like a big pancake. Slice it up like a cake. Cook it in olive oil or duck fat.

Method

1. Boil unpeeled spuds for 10 minutes. Drain. Cool for at least 5 minutes.
2. Peel spuds. Grate coarsely into a bowl. Add salt, pepper, spring onions and dill (if using). Mix lightly using a fork.
3. Heat a little oil and butter or duck fat in a pan. Spoon the spud mix in and spread it out to cover the pan like a pancake.
4. Cook gently for 10 minutes. The underside should be crisp and brown.
5. To turn the rosti, hold a large plate over the pan. Turn both pan and plate over together so that the rosti turns out on to the plate. Then slide it off the plate, back into the pan, browned side up, and cook till brown underneath. Use a light pan which is easy to lift and turn.

For 4
Ingredients

900 g/2lb old potatoes
4 spring onions, thinly sliced (optional)
3 tablespoons chopped fresh dill (optional)
Salt and black pepper
Olive oil plus a knob of butter or duck fat

WHY NOT?

Make the rosti the main event and pile it with bacon and mushrooms, or smoked salmon, or poached or fried eggs.

For 6
Ingredients

450 g/1 lb best-quality minced beef
2 quantities tomato sauce (page 65)
2–3 tablespoons milk
2 thick slices good white bread, crusts removed
Olive/sunflower oil
1 onion, finely chopped
2 garlic cloves, crushed
2.5–5 cm/1–2 in piece fresh root ginger
Plain flour to coat
Grated rind of 1 lemon
2 tablespoons chopped fresh herbs, such as thyme, coriander or parsley
1 egg
Salt and black pepper
Pasta of choice

Eat with: Tagliatelle or other pasta shapes, rice or couscous. Add loads of Parmesan cheese and a sharply dressed salad.

VARIATION
MEATLOAF
Bake the mix in a greased 2 lb/900 g loaf tin at 190°C/375°F/gas 5 for 1–1¼ hours. Scoff hot with tomato sauce (page 65), cold with baked spuds. Great in sandwiches.

Pasta, meatballs & tomato sauce

Back from footie? Meatballs keep the theme going. Put these together before you go out. Stick them in the sauce when you're back in. The beef and ginger idea comes from dim sum Chinese dumplings.

Method

1. Make tomato sauce (page 65).
2. Place bread in large bowl. Add milk. Leave for 5 minutes, then squeeze dry (chuck milk).
3. Heat 1 tablespoon oil in large frying pan. Cook onion and garlic gently, till soft. Add to bread in bowl.
4. Add beef, grated ginger, lemon rind, herbs, egg and salt and pepper to the bread mixture. Mix.
5. Shape meat into walnut-sized balls. Roll lightly in flour.
6. Cook the meatballs gently, in oil for 10–15 minutes, till brown all over, turning now and then.
7. Heat the tomato sauce in a large saucepan. Add meatballs. Reduce heat, cover and cook gently for 15 minutes.

Barbecue mix

Bring on the sun. Eating outside works when mates come round. (No nagging from parents to take off their trainers.) So shoot a few hoops or get in a bit of footie practice while the barbie heats up. If you're not a barbie fan or you don't have one – or it starts to rain – cook all this great stuff inside and eat it wherever you fancy.

A brilliant burger

This one's really worth tasting – not just for filling your face. Use the best mince you can get. (Or blitz your own from steak. Blitzing makes better burgers.)

Method

1. Throw your own blitzed meat or best butcher's mince into a bowl. Season well with salt and pepper. Add finely chopped herbs and lightly beaten egg.
2. Finely chop onion and garlic. Fry in a little olive oil, till soft.
3. Add onion and garlic and stir into the meat. Mix well. Roll into balls then flatten to the size and shape you like.
4. For cooking inside, heat a frying pan or griddle. Cook 3 mins. Turn. Cook for another 3. Repeat till cooked right through. Grill – turning till done – if you prefer.
5. For the barbie – cook for 5 minutes each side on a grill that's 15 cm/6 in from the coals, till done. Toast buns if liked.
6. Slap in buns.

For 4
Ingredients

450 g/1 lb minced beef
Olive oil
1 small onion
2 garlic cloves
3 sprigs fresh thyme, leaves only
1 tablespoon finely chopped fresh parsley
1 small egg, lightly beaten
Salt and black pepper
4 soft white baps

VARIATION

CHEESEBURGERS
Top the cooked burgers with cheese and flash grill to melt.

LAMB PITTA-BURGERS
Use good-quality minced lamb. Add 1 teaspoon ground cumin and chopped fresh coriander instead of thyme and parsley. Serve in warm pitta bread with ketchup and natural yogurt blitzed with garlic, mint and seasoning.

WHY NOT?
Stack burgers with salad, mayo or all your favourite extras.

For 4

Ingredients

450g/1lb fresh tuna
1 good tablespoon Dijon
   mustard
½–1 teaspoon chopped
   pickled ginger for sushi
3 sprigs fresh thyme,
   leaves only (chopped
   dill or coriander are
   also good)
¾ teaspoon fennel
   seeds, ground (use a
   spice grinder or coffee
   grinder)
Pinch of cayenne pepper
Pinch of salt
4 burger buns

Eat with: Dijon mustard,
pickled ginger, garlic
mayo and salad.

Tuna burger

Thanks to the wonder of the tuna burger all your burger needs are solved. It's not dripping in fat, it's not dry. And it's not meat. Tuna's power food. Great if you're into sport. Combo it with ginger and spice. Cook this one inside – take it out for a walk. This is brilliant with sweet potato chips and garlic mayo.

Method

1. Chop tuna into tiny chunks with a sharp knife till it looks like mince. Tip into a bowl with mustard, chopped pickled ginger, fennel, salt, chopped herbs, cayenne. Mix gently to bind.
2. Divide into 4 burger shapes. Chill or use immediately.
3. Put a little oil in a frying pan on a medium heat. Cook the burgers for 3 minutes each side (still a bit pink inside). Turn with care – they're not robust. Don't panic if a bit drops off. Once in the bun it'll all look perfect.

For 4

Ingredients

8 big field mushrooms
Olive oil
Fresh herbs – parsley/
   coriander/thyme
3 garlic cloves, crushed
Salt and black pepper
Lemon juice
Toppings of choice
4 burger buns

Mushroom burger

Don't make this with anything other than the big mushrooms – field or Portobello. Griddle or bake in the oven or on the barbie with herbs and lemon to soup up the taste. Melt cheese over the top if that's what you like – fontina – halloumi – Cheddar. Layer up with your best extras.

Method

1. Preheat oven to 220°C/425°F/gas 7 if cooking inside or place mushroooms on a baking tray if cooking on the barbie.
2. Drizzle with olive oil, squeeze of lemon, salt and pepper, garnish herbs. Leave to marinade for 30 minutes.
3. Bake in the oven for 10 minutes or grill on the barbie for 5–6 or till done.

For 6
Ingredients

900 g/2 lb cubed leg of lamb or lamb fillet
2 sprigs fresh rosemary
2 tablespoons olive oil
1 lemon
Black pepper
Bay leaves for threading

Lamb kebabs

Bring on the rosemary bush. Stick your lamb in a herby marinade overnight to pick up the flavours. Skewer up just before you need it. Chuck more herbs on the fire for the hell of it. Eat kebabs crunchy on the outside – a bit pink in the middle.

VARIATION
SPICY MARINADE FOR THE LAMB
Mix a large pot of natural yogurt, 2 teaspoons each ground cumin and coriander, 2 cloves garlic, lemon juice, chopped rosemary, thyme, or mint. Leave overnight to flavour.

Method

Chuck meat into a bowl with crushed garlic, rosemary leaves, lemon, olive oil. Marinade for 1 hour at least. Divide meat between six flat skewers. Alternate meat with bay leaves. Sprinkle with sea salt. Cook on the barbie. Turn. Baste with marinade. Repeat. Should take 10–12 minutes.

Weekend family meals

Well – you've got to talk to them sometimes, so it might as well be around a table full of food, which puts everyone in a good mood. Sometimes at weekends our kitchen looks like a hurricane's hit it. Everyone's in there. Polly sorting out her veggie thing. Tom and me fixing a roast. Mum fussing – checking her potatoes are done – again. My sisters, Katie and Alice round.

Hopefully at the end of it – if we're still talking – we're all enjoying ourselves sitting at the kitchen table eating. Stuff like **lemon roast chicken with great roast potatoes**. **Herby lamb** cooked straight on the rack, the French way with garlic and herbs. See what's good at the fishmonger and turn it straight into a creamy topped fish pie. **Meaty lasagne** or the veggie version. **Ratatouille**. Dad gets to clean up the kitchen and do the washing up for afters.

For 6
Ingredients

- 1 large chicken (organic free-range is best)
- 2 lemons, 1 for squeezing and 1 cut into chunks
- Rosemary, sage and tarragon sprigs
- 3–4 slices pancetta or rashers streaky bacon
- Olive oil
- Head of garlic, separated into cloves and peeled
- Sea salt and pepper

ROASTIES
- 900 g/2 lb potatoes, (Maris Piper or King Edwards)
- 2 big sweet potatoes, peeled and cut into chunks

Lemon roast chicken
with crisp bacon, garlic, herbs & best roast potatoes

Tom's favourite. He'll text us to make it when he's coming back. It tastes great and looks cool. Don't be put off by cooking a whole bird. Dress it up like a Christmas tree. Roast your spuds in the roasting tin. Whip up a gravy from the lemony juices. Make a top stock from what you've got left. Even the veggie sisters wish they could eat it.

Method

1. Preheat the oven to 190°C/375°F/gas 6.

2. Check the weight of the chicken and calculate the cooking time at 20 minutes per 500 g, plus an additional 20 minutes. Place in a large roasting tin.

3. Drape the pancetta over breast to cover and moisten during cooking. Stick a slice of lemon on top and fix herb sprigs in between joints and all over.

4. Drizzle whole bird with olive oil, lemon, salt and pepper. Slap in the oven. Set timer for your calculated cooking time.

5. In the meantime peel ordinary spuds. Boil for 10 minutes. Drain. Rough up surfaces with a fork to aid crisping. 50 minutes before chicken is done, add potatoes, chunks of peeled sweet potato, lemon chunks and garlic cloves to roasting tin. Squeeze juice over. Season. Put back in oven.

6. When ready, pierce bird with knife to check doneness. Juices must run clear not pink. Remove from oven and leave to rest in warm place for 10–15 minutes.

7. Turn spuds using metal spatula. Shift up in oven or increase temp to crisp up.

8. After 10–15 minutes remove spuds and veg from tin to make gravy. Carve the chicken. Lucky person gets the wishbone. Eat that garlic.

For the gravy: After scooping off excess fat, pour 600 ml/1 pint water into the roasting tin. Put the tin on the hob. Boil hard for 3–4 minutes while stirring and scraping any sticky bits off the bottom of the tin. Taste and season for a thin gravy. Remove. Pour into a jug. Skim off any remaining fat before serving.

Eat with:
Cauliflower cheese (page 71) and crisp green beans.

WINTER
⭐ Cauliflower and broccoli florets are good tossed with chopped garlic, cumin, olive oil and a little salt, then roasted for 30 minutes.
⭐ Cut carrots into sticks, drizzle with orange juice, dot with butter and season. Pack in foil parcels. Bake for 30 minutes.

SUMMER
Great with salads, new potatoes, peas, ratatouille, mayo, chutney and relishes.

For 4–6
Ingredients

1.5 kg/3 lb leg of lamb
Butter
1.5 kg/3 lb potatoes,
  such as Maris Piper or
King Edwards, peeled
  and thinly sliced
8 garlic cloves, sliced
Fresh herb sprigs –
  rosemary, mint, thyme
  or sage
Olive oil
Salt and black pepper

Eat with: Green beans.
Green salad. Mint sauce.
Ratatouille.

VARIATION
Roast lamb in a tin.
At STEP 2 press a
sharp knife into the
lamb. Push garlic and
herbs down into the
meat. Repeat a few
times. Put the lamb
into a tin. Drizzle with
oil and salt. Surround
with part boiled
potatoes. Roast
together till done.

Slashed roast herby lamb
with garlic potatoes

Tasty and slightly weird – a roast without a tin. Prep the meat. Stick it directly on the top shelf of your oven. Make up a dish of sliced garlic potatoes to sit on the shelf underneath and catch the juices. A great eat – saves on washing up. Treat the family.

Method

1. Preheat the oven to 200°C/400°F/gas 6.
2. Grease a large, shallow ovenproof dish with lots of butter. Layer the potatoes in the dish, adding half the garlic, dots of butter and seasoning.
3. Make deep, wide diamond shape slashes over the lamb. Stick the remaining garlic into the slashes with sprigs of herbs. Place the lamb on a plate. Season well. Drizzle with oil.
4. Put dish of potatoes on to the lower shelf in the oven. Carry the lamb to oven on its plate. Then slip it straight on to the top shelf directly over the spuds.
5. Roast for 1½ hours. The meat gets a bit crunchy and opens up cooked this way. Test by piercing with a sharp knife – still a bit pink is fine but cook longer for well-done meat, to taste.
6. Leave lamb to relax on a plate somewhere warm for 15–20 minutes. Shift spuds to the top shelf to brown and crisp. Whack up the heat if you think it needs it.

Ratatouille Nicoise

Check out the full-on flavour of this cool veg stew. There's a sweet-sour kick in there which keeps the sisters sweet. It's got enough personality to work on its own but it's great as a team player with lamb.

Method

1. Heat some olive oil in a large casserole. Lightly brown the aubergines. Drain on kitchen paper.

2. Add more oil. Cook the onion and celery till lightly browned. Add the tomatoes, courgettes, vinegar, sugar, salt and lemon. Cook very gently for 15 minutes, stirring to prevent sticking.

3. Increase heat. Replace aubergines. Add the capers, olives and thyme. Simmer for 10 minutes or till the veg are tender. Taste: add more sugar or vinegar, or seasoning if you like.

For 4–6

Ingredients

3 aubergines, cut into chunks
1 onion, thinly sliced
2 celery sticks, sliced
3–4 large ripe tomatoes, quartered and seeded
2 courgettes, cut into chunks
Olive oil
2 tablespoons wine vinegar
1 tablespoon sugar
1 small lemon wedge
2 teaspoons capers
8 black olives
Fresh thyme sprigs
Salt and black pepper

For 4
Ingredients

900 g/2 lb white fish
   fillet or use up to
   225 g/ 8 oz salmon or
   smoked haddock
600 ml/1 pint milk
75 g/3 oz butter
50 g/2 oz plain flour
3 tablespoons chopped
   fresh parsley or dill
½ teaspoon mustard
Squeeze of lemon
1 small onion
75 g/3 oz mushrooms,
   sliced
3 eggs, hard-boiled
   (optional)
100 g/4 oz peeled
   cooked prawns
   (optional)
Salt and pepper

POTATO TOPPING
900 g/2 lb potatoes, cut
   into chunks
4 tablespoons milk
Knob of butter, plus
   extra for topping
½ teaspoon mustard
50 g/2 oz cheese,
   grated (optional)

Eat with: Mushy peas,
green beans.

Fisherman's pie

When my mate Fordy and I go fishing we never know
what we're about to catch. Bit like this pie. Make it
different each time. Use basically white fish (see
what's about), then sub in a bit of salmon, prawns
and a bit of smoked haddock.

Method

1. Preheat the oven to 200°C/400°F/gas 6. Slap fish and milk in
a large ovenproof dish. Bake for 10 minutes.
2. For topping, boil potatoes for 15–20 minutes. Drain. Mash
with milk, butter, mustard, lemon and seasoning.
3. Transfer the fish to a plate. Save milk. Peel skin from fish. Cut
the flesh into chunks. Remove any bones.
4. Melt 2 oz of the butter in a pan. Add flour. Stir and cook
gently for 2 minutes. Gradually stir in the reserved milk. Boil,
stirring, to make a smooth, thick white sauce (see page 155 for
method). Add seasoning, herbs, mustard and lemon juice.
5. Lightly fry onion in remaining butter. Add mushrooms. Cook
for 2 minutes.
6. Put fish, mushroom mix, halved eggs and prawns (if using)
in the dish. Cover with the sauce. Top with mash. Rough top up
with fork. Dot with bits of butter or grated cheese.
7. Bake for 30–40 minutes.

VARIATION

MAGNIFICENT MOUSSAKA
Add a pinch of cinnamon to your meat sauce. Fry up thin slices of 2–3 aubergines. Layer up meat, aubergine, sauce in a dish. Finish with aubergine and cheese sauce. Bake as you would lasagne.

Lasagne

Flat pack pasta. This one behaves itself. Layer it up with a totally tasty meat sauce and cheese sauce. It bakes in the oven with no fuss. Make double if everyone's got friends staying for the weekend. In which case they really owe you.

Method

1. Prepare the Bolognese sauce.

2. Preheat the oven to 200°C/400°F/gas 6. Grease a large lasagne dish or oblong ovenproof dish at least 5 cm/2 in deep.

3. Make the white sauce and stir in the grated Cheddar cheese, mustard and lemon juice.

4. Spread one third of the meat sauce in the dish. Add a single layer of pasta. Drizzle with a little cheese sauce. Sprinkle with a little Parmesan. Add another third of meat, another layer of pasta, and a little cheese sauce. Then the last of the meat and a final layer of pasta. Top with the remaining cheese sauce.

5. Dot with butter or sprinkle with mozzarella, Cheddar or Parmesan cheese. Bake for 40 minutes.

6. Remove from the oven and let the lasagne relax for 10 minutes before serving.

For 6–8
Ingredients

1 quantity Bolognese sauce (page 64)

1 quantity Basic white sauce (page 155)

75 g/6 oz mature Cheddar cheese, grated

½–1 teaspoon English mustard

Juice of ½ lemon

250 g/9 oz pack no-pre-cook lasagne

4–6 tablespoons freshly grated Parmesan cheese

About 25 g/1 oz butter or 100 g/4 oz mozzarella cheese, sliced or 50 g/2 oz Cheddar or Parmesan cheese, grated (for top)

VARIATION

VEGGIE LASAGNE
At STEP 1 make ratatouille or griddle up a plate of veg. At STEP 4 use ratatouille or griddled veg with home made tomato sauce (page 65) instead of meat sauce. Bake. Delicious.

Puddings...

Puddings? Eat them. They're the best bit. They keep the family quiet. Bring one in and they all shut up – reach for the spoons and get stuck in there. Puddings make everyday mealtimes feel pretty cool. They can cheer up even the worst kind of day.

Short on time? Blitz up a yogurt with something sparky. Dice a fruit salad. More time? Take **chocolate roulade** – a big slice. **Chocolate mousse** – my personal favourite.

Use the pudding course to sharpen your cooking skills. Whip up a **treacle tart**. Classic. Fling **meringues** together. Smash them up for **Eton mess**. Make tangy **lemon souffle cream pudding**. Drown **sliced oranges in caramel sauce**. Treat yourself to **tutti-fruity crumble** pud. Slice up a **cheesecake** when you've loads of people around. Turn out my mate Tom's amazing **amaretti surprise**. Never eat **ice-cream** without one of our storming **home-style sauces**.

VARIATION

THAI LIME FRUIT SALAD
Like your fruit syrupy? Boil 300 ml/½ pt water, 125 g/4 oz sugar, 5 dried lime leaves and 1 stick lemongrass for 5 minutes. Cool. Add juice of a lime. Strain. Add chopped exotic fruit. Chill.

FRUIT SALAD
No skewers? Chuck the fruit in a bowl. Drizzle with a little fresh orange/apple juice. Chill.

For 4

Ingredients

Small bunch seedless grapes – red or green, or mixed
Punnet of strawberries,
1 star fruit
2 kiwi fruit, skinned
1 small pineapple
½ galia melon
1 slice watermelon
1 mango
1 apple or pear
Lemon juice

Fruit kebabs

Put a bowl of whole fruit on the table. What happens? People ignore it. Chop up the same fruit – stick it on skewers and they get excited. Strange. Use any fruit you like for this. Include a few exotics for special occasions. For everyday, just see what's hanging around. Even a pear or an apple can look cool skewered.

Method

1. Keep grapes and strawberries whole.
2. Slice and deseed melons. Cut into chunks.
3. Peel and chunk pineapple, mango and kiwi. Slice star fruit stars.
4. Peel and chop apple or pear. Brush with lemon to stop browning.
5. Thread up in any order on 8 wooden skewers.

My mate Tom's amaretti surprise

Cool souffle? Hot meringue with a fruity sauce? Try it.

Method

1. Preheat oven to 180°C/350°F/gas 4. Spread butter all over the inside of a 800 ml/1½ pint souffle dish. Tip extra sugar in. Roll round to coat. Tip out excess.

2. Whisk egg whites, salt and cream of tartar in a large bowl with an electric or hand whisk till holding soft peaks. Whisk sugar in bit by bit till the mix is really thick. Gently fold in half the biscuit with a metal spoon.

3. Scoop mix gently into dish. Bake for 20 minutes. It rises so leave room.

4. Serve in the dish before it sinks. Pour on sauce. Sprinkle with biscuit. Or let it settle for a few minutes. Run a knife round the edge. Invert carefully onto a plate. Sprinkle biscuit. Surround with sauce. Or chill then serve as before. Delicious.

For 6–8

Ingredients

4 large egg whites
Good pinch of salt
Good pinch of cream of tartar
50 g/2 oz caster sugar
1 tablespoon soft butter
1 tablespoon caster sugar for coating dish
8 crisp amaretti biscuits, roughly crushed
1 quantity Raspberry sauce (page 130)

Chocolate mousse

For 4–6

Ingredients

175 g/6 oz good-quality dark plain chocolate

2 tablespoons strong black coffee (use a good teaspoon of instant coffee to make half a mug)

4 large eggs

1 tablespoon butter at room temperature

2 teaspoons orange juice or rum (optional)

People have been known to walk out of our house carrying pots of this chocolate mousse. But not if I get to them first. It's quick and easy to make. Eat it from one big dish, in glasses, tea cups, or ramekin dishes. Don't bother about piling fruit or cream on top. It's simply chocolatey. Get your spoon in there.

Method

1. Separate the eggs. Put yolks in one large bowl, whites in another.

2. One-third fill a saucepan with water. Bring to a very gentle simmer. Find a heatproof bowl to fit the pan without touching the water. Break the chocolate into the bowl. Add the coffee.

3. Sit the bowl of chocolate on the pan. Let it soften slowly – too fast and hot and it spoils.

4. Watch the chocolate melt into the coffee. Stir round twice with a wooden spoon to combine. Take off heat. Work fast. Tip into yolks. Stir in.

5. Add the butter and rum or orange juice. Beat fast and furious till glossy.

6. Whisk the egg whites with a pinch of salt till white and stiff but not dry. Tip into chocolate.

7. Fold the whites and chocolate together using a big metal spoon and figure-of-eight movements. Don't overwork – keep the air in. The odd spot of white doesn't matter.

8. Spoon mix into dishes or cups. Chill for a couple of hours or longer. Delicious.

Tutti-fruity crumble

This is nothing like bad school crumble.

Method

1. Preheat the oven to 180°C/350°F/gas 4.

2. Peel, core and slice the apples. Throw them into a pan with half the sugar, the butter, orange juice and water. Put on low heat for about 5 minutes. Turn the fruit with a wooden spoon as it softens a little.

3. Tip apples into a 1.2 litre/2 pint dish. Add the other fruit. Sprinkle the rest of the sugar over and mix.

4. For the crumble, tip flour into a bowl. Cut the butter into smallish bits. Chuck in with flour. Using your fingertips, rub butter into the flour till the mix looks crumbly and a bit lumpy still. Throw in the sugar. Mix.

5. Spread the topping lightly over fruit – don't press it down.

6. Bake for 30–35 minutes, till fruit cooked and crumble golden.

For 4

Ingredients

2–3 dessert apples
2 tablespoons sugar
2 teaspoons butter
Squeeze of orange juice
2 tablespoons water
1 banana, sliced
100 g/4 oz raspberries
1 peach, peeled and
  sliced

CRUMBLE TOPPING
175g/6 oz plain flour
75 g/3 oz cold butter
75 g/3 oz caster sugar

Eat with: Cream, custard or ice-cream.

Makes 8

Ingredients

4 large eggs – use the whites only
225 g/8 oz caster sugar
300 ml/½ pint double cream
450 g/1 lb raspberries

VARIATION

PAVLOVA
At STEP 6 use a spatula to shape all the mixture into one big flat meringue. Cook for 1½ hours. Then allow to get cold. Pile it high with raspberries and cream when cold.

MERINGUE GLACE
Sandwich 2 meringue shells together with cream and ice-cream. Drizzle with chocolate or butterscotch sauce. Eat with chopped fresh peach and sliced banana.

For 4–6

Ingredients

300 ml/½ pint double cream
8 meringues
450 g/1 lb strawberries
Good drizzle white wine or orange juice
25 g/1 oz icing sugar

Meringue shells
with raspberries and cream

Everyone knows what a meringue is. This is just the best way of doing it.

Method

1. Preheat oven to 150°C/300°F/gas 2.

2. Grease a large flat baking tray with oil. Line it with non-stick baking paper. Wash hands – any grease stops whites successfully whisking.

3. Separate the eggs. Put the whites into a large bowl or the bowl of the mixer. Save your yolks for making mayo.

4. Whisk the whites till foamy then add the sugar – a tablespoon at a time whisking in between. Keep going till the mix is glossy and thick.

5. Scoop meringue up with a tablespoon. Use another to help get it onto the baking tray in a traditional meringue shape. Tease the meringue into a good uneven blob. Repeat – leaving space for the meringues to expand.

6. Reduce oven heat to 140°C/275°F/gas 1. Cook meringues for 1½ hours. Turn the heat off. Leave the meringues to dry out as the oven cools.

7. Peel them off the paper carefully. They'll keep in a tin for up to a week. Sandwich together with whipped cream for eating. Chuck on some fresh raspberries.

Eton mess

Buy in meringues to make this great pud. It's pointless making your own then breaking them to bits. Unless you've got loads left over.

Method

1. Roughly chop strawberries. Chuck in a bowl. Splash with orange juice or wine to soak. Add icing sugar. Chill for a bit.

2. Just before eating, whisk cream till soft (not rock hard).

3. Crunch up meringues. Chuck them into the cream. Add fruit. Stir gently for cool marbly effect.

4. Spoon into glasses, tumblers or big bowl. Get in there.

VARIATION
Use all raspberries or mix half and half with strawberries. Crush a few raspberries and use the rest whole.

For 6
Ingredients

SHORTCRUST PASTRY
225 g/8 oz plain flour
100 g/4 oz cold butter
2–3 tablespoons very cold water

FILLING
Grated rind of 1 lemon
1 tablespoon lemon juice
9 tablespoons fresh white breadcrumbs
9 tablespoons golden syrup
3 tablespoons double cream

Treacle tart

Try making your own shortcrust pastry for this one. It doesn't take much time. And once you're down with the method – which is dead simple – you'll be throwing this stuff together in just a few minutes.

Method

1. Grease a 23 cm/9 in tart tin.
2. Stir flour into a bowl. Cut butter into small bits and rub gently into the flour with fingertips till the butter disappears into the flour. It should look like fine breadcrumbs – no lumps.
3. Add 2 tablespoons of water. Mix with a fork. Add a splash more water if needed. Draw the pastry into a ball using your fingers. Be cool. Going easy makes great pastry.
4. Sit pastry on a floured board. Roll it out gently with a floured rolling pin. Go for 5 mm/¼ in thick. It needs to make a shape that is big enough to cover the base and sides of the tin, plus a bit extra.
5. Slip the rolling pin under the pastry. Hold it over the tin and unroll the pastry into it. If it's not perfect don't worry – use bits of pastry to fill gaps and fake it.
6. Roll the pin over the top to cut off overhanging pastry.
7. Prick base of tart lightly all over with fork. Put into fridge for 30 minutes.
8. Preheat oven to 190°C/375°F/ gas 5. Mix breadcrumbs, syrup, cream, lemon rind and juice. Pour into pastry case. Bake for 25–30 minutes till golden. Eat warm. Great cold. Try with custard or ice-cream.

Lemon souffle cream pudding

If you're a lemon fan you'll go for this. It doesn't look special. But it's got two surprises. A soft sponge top which melts in the mouth. And a layer of creamy lemon sauce at the bottom.

Method

1. Preheat oven to 180°C/350°F/gas 4. Grease a 1.5 litre/2½ pint pie or souffle dish.

2. Separate eggs. Put whites in a large bowl and whisk till they form stiff peaks.

3. Use a wooden spoon or hand-held electric beater to cream butter and sugar till creamy and light. Add lemon rind then juice. May look odd but keep beating.

4. Whisk in beaten egg yolks bit by bit. Add flour. Beat. Pour in milk. Mix. Fold in egg whites.

5. Pour into dish. Sit dish in a roasting tin. Pour hot water into tin till it comes halfway up the outside of the dish.

6. Bake for 40–50 minutes or till risen and golden brown on top. Eat hot, warm or cold.

For 4
Ingredients

4 lemons
5 medium eggs
125 g/4 oz soft butter
175 g/6 oz caster sugar
60 g/2 oz plain flour
120 ml/¼ pint milk

WHY NOT?

Stick lemons into your oven for a couple of minutes before squeezing. You'll get more juice out of them.

For 8–10
Ingredients

225 g/8 oz ginger or
  digestive biscuits
75 g/3 oz butter
675 g/1½ lb curd cheese
  or cream cheese
175 g/6 oz caster sugar
3 eggs
1 lemon
Few drops vanilla extract
Chinese gooseberries,
  strawberries or
  raspberries

Our fave cheesecake

This baked cheesecake is great if you've got mates over. Or loads of family about. It's got a smooth texture and a cool ginger-biscuit base. Pile it up with whatever fruit you fancy. I like it plain with Chinese gooseberries. They've got a great look and fizz to them.

Method

1. Preheat oven to 150°C/300°F/gas 2. Use butter to grease a round 23 cm/9 inch loose-bottomed cake tin.

2. Stick biscuits in a freezer bag. Bash with a rolling pin till they're in fine crumbs. Or blitz in a processor.

3. Melt butter in pan. Add crumbs. Stir to mix. Tip into the cake tin. Press evenly to cover. Firm up in fridge.

4. Tip cheese, caster sugar, eggs, lemon rind, vanilla extract and good squeeze of lemon into processor. Blitz briefly till just smooth. (No machine? Beat together with a wooden spoon.)

5. Pour cheesecake to cover biscuit base. Bake for 35–40 minutes. Turn off oven. Leave cake in there to cool and firm up. Chill for 2 hours at least.

6. Stick fruit in to decorate. Or cover with whipped cream and pile with fruit of choice.

Sliced oranges in caramel syrup

Oranges make a great end to a meal. Eat them sliced up in caramel sauce. It's a bit posh. Enjoy the sound effects.

Method

1. Peel and thinly slice the oranges. Put them in a bowl with any spilled juice.

2. Put 150 ml cold water and caster sugar in a heavy bottomed pan with lemongrass or rosemary. Put on a low heat. Leave to dissolve until transparent. Stir with a wooden spoon.

3. Turn up the heat. No more stirring. Allow the sugar water to boil up fiercely for a few minutes until it turns golden brown.

4. Have a jug with 150 ml of hot water standing by.

5. Wear oven gloves for the next bit and take major care. Carry the pan of caramel over to the sink very carefully. Hold the pan well away from your face – over the sink – prepare for the sound of fireworks as you pour the water slowly into the hot sugar mix to dilute.

6. Pour the sauce over the oranges and leave to cool. Chill.

For 4–6
Ingredients

6 oranges

SYRUP
225 g/8 oz caster sugar
1 stick lemongrass/large
  sprig of rosemary
150 ml/¼ pint cold water
  for dissolving sugar
150 ml/¼ pint hot water
  for thinning caramel

VARIATION
Good mixed with grapefruit or grapefruit alone.

For 8–10
Ingredients

Sunflower oil, for
  greasing
225 g/8 oz dark plain
  chocolate
150 g/5 oz caster sugar
5 eggs
1 teaspoon instant coffee
4½ tablespoons water
Icing sugar
300 ml/½–¾ pint double
  cream

Eat with: Fresh berries.

WHY NOT?
Make the base the
night before. Fill and
eat the next day.

Chocolate roulade

A bit of a legend in our house. I can't explain why. Just make it and taste it. Rolling a roulade and getting it on to the plate in one piece is a bit of a mission. But even if it cracks up it really doesn't matter. It'll taste great. Special enough for a birthday party.

Method

1. Preheat the oven to 220°C/425°F/gas 7. Grease a Swiss roll tin measuring 23 x 33 cm/9 x 13 in with oil. Cut a sheet of greaseproof paper big enough to line and stand above the rim of the tin by 4 cm/1½ in all around. Fold the paper to fit the corners, fit it into the tin and grease very lightly with oil.

2. Separate the eggs using oil free hands. Yolks in one large bowl and whites in another.

3. Tip the caster sugar in with the yolks. Whisk together till light, pale and moussey using an electric or hand whisk.

4. Break the chocolate into a heavy bottomed pan. Add water and coffee granules.

5. Put pan on a <u>very</u> low heat and stir gently with a wooden spoon till creamy and melted.

6. Fold the melted chocolate into the mousse using a large metal spoon.

7. Whisk the egg whites till well frothy and almost stiff. Fold gently into the chocolate mix. The odd spot of white doesn't matter.

8. Pour the mix into the tin. Cook for 12–14 minutes – roulade should look browned and may be cracked on top. It will sink when you take it out. Leave to cool.

9. Whisk the double cream till softly firm. Smooth it over the roulade with a palette knife.

10. Lift the short end of the roulade and roll it up away from you so it looks like an odd Swiss roll. Peel off the backing paper as you roll. It may crack and bits may come away. Don't panic – keep going. When it's nearly there and the paper just hanging on lift the whole thing onto a plate.

11. Sprinkle with a little sifted icing sugar.

Storming sauces

Here are four great sauces to eat with ice-cream. Just pour them over or make up a sundae with fresh fruit, meringue and maybe a sparkler.

Best chocolate sauce

For 6
Ingredients
- 100 g/4 oz dark plain chocolate
- 15 g/½ oz butter
- 2 tablespoons water
- 2 tablespoons golden syrup
- 1 teaspoon natural vanilla essence

Method
1. Break the chocolate into bowl. Place over a pan of simmering water.
2. Add butter, syrup and water. Melt and stir till smooth.
3. Remove from heat and add the essence. Serve hot over ice-cream. Will store covered in fridge for a week.

Butterscotch sauce

For 6
Ingredients
- 25 g/1 oz butter
- 2 tablespoons golden syrup
- 175 g/6 oz soft brown sugar
- 4 tablespoons single cream

Method
Melt butter, golden syrup and sugar together in a small pan. Bring to the boil. Stir in the cream then re-heat gently. Will store as above. Delicious hot or cold.

Raspberry sauce

For 6
Ingredients
- 225 g/8 oz raspberries
- 1–2 tablespoons caster sugar

Method
Put raspberries into pan with a little sugar. Heat gently till they soften and release their juices. Sieve over a bowl. Pour over ice-cream or use in making a sundae.

Mars bar sauce
Method
Break the Mars bar up into pieces in a small pan. Tip in the milk. Mix with a wooden spoon till smooth but with bits of caramel. Pour over ice-cream while warm.

For 2
Ingredients
1 Mars bar
3 tablespoons milk

Party,
party, party

Shindigs? I love them. Birthday, sleepover, disco, movie marathon, school's out, year's over, mates over, music – whatever. Eating. Crisps are OK – but hey – it's a party. So make up yourself industrial amounts of small food. **Quarter burgers**. Slices of your own **pizza**. **Big chips and chilli. Baked nachos with salsa, guacamole and Cheddar. Crisp thin crostini** with cool toppings. **Baked sticky chicken**. Plates piled with **cheese skewers**. Slap out some **best bangers with honey and mustard. Popcorn**.

Choc up some **fresh fruit**. Tower up a load of **mini meringues**. Whip up big bowls of **choc mousse**. Make up **fruit kebabs.** Stuff **oranges or lemon shells with lemon sorbet**.

Prep stuff ahead so you can get out there and chill. Got people staying over? Check there's stuff in the fridge for a brilliant breakfast.

Quarter burgers

These'll keep you dancing. Quarter versions of the real thing impaled on cocktail sticks.

Makes 16

Ingredients

1 quantity Brilliant burgers (page 103)
4 burger buns

EXTRAS
Tomato ketchup
Mayo
Slices of gherkin
Mustard
Rocket (optional)

Method

1. Make mix. Divide into burgers. Flatten into pattie shapes and chill till needed.
2. Cook as usual. Lightly toast buns. Stack with a few extras.
3. Divide each burger into four. Secure with cocktail sticks.

Party pizza slices

Make up loadsa pizza bases. Freeze. Top with your best combos. Wear coolest clothes for serving...

Makes 16 slices

Ingredients

7 g sachet fast-action easy blend yeast or 25 g/1 oz fresh yeast
300 ml/½ pint warm water
450 g/1 lb strong white flour
1 teaspoon salt
2 tablespoons olive oil

Method

1. Sieve flour and salt into a warm bowl.
2. If using fresh yeast, mix with a little of the warm water.
3. Tip either fresh yeast mix or easy blend yeast, olive oil and remaining water into flour. Mix to a dough. Knead on a floured board for 8 minutes till smooth and springy.
4. Leave to rise in a warm place for 1 hour or till doubled in size in a large covered bowl. Lightly oil four baking trays.
5. Knead briefly. Cut dough into four. Roll into circles or rectangles to fit baking trays.
6. Leave covered on baking trays to rise again for 15–20 minutes.
7. Choose basic topping (see page 83) and cook at once in a preheated oven at 230°C/450°F/gas 8. Bake for 15–20 minutes, or do the bases ahead. Freeze uncovered on trays. When hard, store in freezer bags till party time. Top and cook whilst frozen.

Sticky chicken

Sticky wings or drumsticks? Both would work – do one quantity of each with double the dose of marinade.

Method

1. Heat honey, pineapple juice, wine vinegar and soy gently in a pan. Add garlic, ginger, spring onions, sesame seeds and sesame oil. Stir well. Remove. Cool.

2. Slap chicken in dish. Pour over honey mix. Turn. Leave in fridge for at least 2 hours or overnight.

3. Preheat oven to 200°C/400°F/gas 6. Put chicken in roasting tin. Squeeze over lemon or lime juice and turn in marinade. Cook for 35–40 minutes, turning two or three times. Great hot, warm or cold.

For 12
Ingredients

3 tablespoons honey
50 ml/2 fl oz pineapple juice
1 tablespoon white or red wine vinegar
50 ml/2 fl oz soy sauce
2 garlic cloves, crushed
5 cm/2 in piece fresh root ginger, grated
3 spring onions, finely chopped
4 teaspoons sesame oil
900 g/2 lb chicken wings
Sesame seeds

Party baked nachos

Something with a bit of bite. Get around the table with people you like…

Method

1. Preheat the oven to 180°C/350°F/gas 4.

2. Lay chips out on baking trays. Top with a bit of salsa. Sprinkle with grated cheddar. Bake for 5–10 minutes. Done when cheese bubbles.

3. Serve with sour cream, guacamole and lime for squeezing.

For 12
Ingredients

3 big packs tortilla chips
Double quantity Salsa (page 80)
225 g/8 oz strong Cheddar cheese, grated
300 ml/½ pint sour cream
Double quantity Guacamole (page 80)
3 limes, cut into wedges

For 10

Ingredients

400 g/14 oz feta cheese
  (2 packs)
4 tablespoons olive oil
1 tablespoon lemon juice
1 teaspoon dried
  oregano
1 cucumber
20 cherry tomatoes
20 seedless grapes
10 pitted black olives

Greek salad skewers

Go global with cheeses on sticks. Use cocktail sticks or wooden skewers to thread up three sorts of cheeses with great extras. Pop your balloons with them after...

Method

1. Cube up the cheese. Marinade in a little oil, lemon juice and oregano. Toss and leave for 30 minutes.
2. Peel and cube cucumber. Thread ingredients onto skewers or cocktail sticks if cheese is crumbly.

VARIATION

ENGLISH
COCKTAIL STICKS
Cheddar, pineapple chunks, grapes and celery.

ITALIAN SKEWERS
Mini balls of mozzarella, cherry tomatoes, basil leaves and olives.

Exam Tip SIX Eat omega 3s

Ultimate brain boosters. Find them in oily fish, such as salmon, fresh tuna, mackerel, sardines and anchovies. They get you thinking sharp and fast and chill you out. So cook up a tasty fish main meal or snack.

Smoked salmon bagel

One of my favourites. An eating classic. Have a pack of salmon in the fridge. Defrost a bagel. Keep it simple or pile it with extras – why not scrambled a couple of eggs. Pile on the bagel before adding the salmon, with a slice of tomato and rocket leaves.

Ingredients:
1 bagel
Low-fat soft cheese
2 slices smoked salmon
Sliced avocado (optional)
Rocket (optional)
Lemon juice
Black pepper
Method:
1. Split the bagel. Spread with soft cheese.
2. Top with salmon. Layer up with avocado and rocket (if using). Squeeze lemon over. Season with plenty of black pepper. Mmmm.

Exam Tip SEVEN Snack on the right stuff

When you're stressed out snacks can do it. You'll want to be eating small things at odd times. So get stuff that keeps you going and works for you while you're taking time out. Like dips and crudites. A tasty wrap or sandwich. Toasted fruit bread and peanut butter. Sometimes I make up a plate of bits like nuts, dates, sunflower and pumpkin seeds, raisins, chopped fresh fruit and veg, and orange segments sprinkled with cinnamon. Or I head down to the kitchen to make a snack and give myself a break – stroke the cat – watch a bit of a funny video.

Rice cakes with guacamole & Cheddar

Is it a snack? Is it a chilling brain-boost? It's both.
FOR 1
Ingredients:
1 portion Guacamole (page 80)
2–3 rice cakes

Tasty Cheddar
Method:
1. Blitz up your guacamole.
2. Spread on rice cakes and grate cheese on top.
VARIATION: Why not spread crispbread with butter and vegemite. Top with grated Cheddar or cottage cheese.

Banana, cheese & honey muffin

This one works. It's sweet and delicious.
Ingredients:
1 muffin
Honey
Ricotta or cottage cheese
1 banana
Method:
1. Slice muffin across. Toast.
2. Drizzle honey. Top with a dollop of cheese and sliced banana.
VARIATION: CINNAMON BANANA MUFFIN
At STEP 2 cream some butter, honey and gound cinnamon together. Top with sliced banana.

Exam Tip EIGHT Take time out to exercise

Move. Exercise is the best stress buster on the planet. And anything goes. Press-ups. Go for a run around the block. Get out the  punchbag. Work out to some music in your room. Even getting up to have a stretch helps. Walking about clears the brain and makes you feel better. If you're frozen at your desk lift your shoulders up to your ears, then drop them right down three times – breathe out as you do it.

Learn to breathe deeply

Check this out. It works. My mum teaches this exercise to actors and TV presenters who get really nervous, and to people who are feeling really stressed about stuff. Try it while you're revising – it helps you think better. Have it as your emergency strategy to get you through spoken exams and to get you going if you panic. What it does is whack loads of oxygen to your brain to bring your adrenalin levels down. And stop your mind going blank – not useful when you turn over that exam paper.

Here's how to do it. Stand in front of a big mirror. Put your hands on your hips. Now move them up to find the bottom of your ribcage. Put slight pressure on the ribs. Now take a deep, silent breath in through your nose. As you do it, make the ribs push out against your hands so the rib cage is expanding sideways – not pulling up. When the ribs have expanded as much as they can, then let them come back slowly into position again. You may get a bit of a rush to the head so stop if you need to. Now breathe out steadily through your mouth at the same time to a count of 15 in your head. Repeat three or four times. You should feel really calm and chilled out…

When you're down with the method, do it without your hands there. Do it in exams or waiting for an oral. Do it when you're in bed to help you sleep.

Exam Tip NINE Sleep

Get loads of sleep. It's the ultimate stress release. But hard if you're uptight or if the exam's next day. So if counting sheep doesn't work try breathing. As you're lying in bed, take deep breaths down to the bottom of your stomach. Imagine the air's filling it like a balloon. Then let the air out slowly again. Repeat a few times. This should clear your mind and calm you. Caffeine could be the problem if you're not sleeping – check that out. Eat to chill out in the evening – stuff like pasta's great. Try Spaghetti alla carbonara (page 66). Make yourself a milky drink before bed.

Pre-exam night hot chocolate

Treat yourself the night before an exam. This hot chocolate works. Froth the top. Delicious.

Ingredients:

Large mug of milk or milk and water

50 g/2 oz dark plain chocolate

Method:

1. Put water and milk or milk into a pan on a gentle heat.

2. Add broken up bits of chocolate.

3. Stir for 3–4 minutes, or until it melts. Use the time to relax.

4. Froth chocolate with hand blender or whisk. Pour into mug.

5. Go to bed. Drink. Sleep.

Exam Tip TEN

Eat tactically on exam days

Give yourself all the help you can. Don't try eating or drinking anything new. Don't OD on coffee. Take water into the exams.

FOR MORNING EXAMS: Have breakfast – baked beans on toast, egg and toast, fruit, yogurt or a banana-based smoothie if you can't face anything solid.

FOR AFTERNOON EXAMS: Nothing too heavy – you'll get dopey. Eat a light soup with a bit of bread and fruit. Or a wrap or sarnie with a lean meat or light veggie filling. For speaking exams: eat really light food. No coffee – it dries the throat and makes you more nervous. No dairy – it clogs up your throat. Sip water before you go in. Sit and do some light breathing exercises.

Essential Extras

Sort out some basic techniques and brilliant eats. These extras make all the difference. Make your own breads, mayo, dressings, stocks and other essentials. Get hooked on real flavours. Do it.

Salads need dressing

Even a bit of sad lettuce gets the star treatment with one of these dressings. Try them all out. See what you like. The trick is to match your basic salad flavours and textures with the type of dressing.

Our everyday French dressing

This makes a great basic dressing. Sometimes we just whisk everything together in a bowl (vinegar and mustard first – oil last). Other times we put it in a jar and shake it.

Ingredients:
1 teaspoon English or Dijon mustard
1 teaspoon caster sugar
1 clove garlic, crushed (optional)
2 tablespoons wine vinegar (red, white or sherry type)
6 tablespoons olive oil
½ shallot, chopped (optional)
Chopped parsley (optional)
Salt and black pepper
Method:
1. Stick mustard, sugar, salt, pepper, garlic (if using) and vinegar in a jar.
2. Slap on the lid. Shake till it's thick and comes together.
3. Add oil. Shake again. Add shallot and parsley, if using.

A great honey & mustard dressing

Feel free to add other extras to basic dressings. You could use cider vinegar here. Or a bit of walnut oil (really good for you by the way). This one has a lovely sweet-sharp flavour.

Ingredients:
2 teaspoons wholegrain mustard
1 teaspoon honey
1 garlic clove, crushed
2 tablespoons lemon juice or white wine vinegar
6 tablespoons olive oil
Salt and black pepper
Method:
1. Tip mustard, honey, seasoning, garlic, lemon juice or vinegar into a jar. Close and shake.
2. Add olive oil. Shake again.

Italian hands-on dressing

Smash this one together. Throw it on to the leaves. Mix with your hands so it's well coated. Good, sharp and tasty.

Ingredients:
1 garlic clove
1 teaspoon balsamic vinegar
5 teaspoons sherry vinegar
2 tablespoons olive oil
Salt
Method:
1. Smash the garlic clove to a paste with the side of a knife on a board or in a mortar with a pestle. Add salt.
2. Put in a bowl or leave in the mortar. Add the vinegars and pinch of sugar.
3. Drizzle oil over the leaves. Add the vinegar-garlic mix.

Home express dressing

Take your olive oil and wine vinegar to the table. Drizzle oil on first. Then a bit of vinegar.

On a diet? Eat yogurt

Blitz low-fat natural yogurt, herbs, garlic and seasoning.

Oriental-style dressing

This one's got a bit of a fizz. Use it all over the place, not just with oriental-style stuff.

Ingredients:
75 ml/3 fl oz sunflower oil
1 teaspoon sesame oil
4½ teaspoons wine vinegar
1 tablespoon soy sauce
1 small shallot, chopped
2.5 cm/1 in piece fresh root ginger grated or pinch of ground ginger
Method:
Whisk the lot together.

Home-made mayo

It's science. All these random ingredients getting together in a brilliant creamy mayo. Make the basic then go with the options.

Ingredients:
2 egg yolks
½ teaspoon each of salt, dry mustard and caster sugar
250 ml/8 fl oz sunflower or groundnut oil
50 ml/2 fl oz olive oil
2 tablespoons white wine vinegar or lemon juice
1 tablespoon hot water
Method:
1. Chuck the egg yolks into a bowl. Add salt, mustard and sugar. Beat till smooth with a balloon whisk. Sit the bowl on a tea towel to stop it slipping.
2. Mix the oils in a jug. Pour the oil, drip by drip, on to the eggs, whisking all the time. Keep it slow to start, so the mix won't curdle. After a bit it'll start to thicken.
3. When you've used half the oil, stop. Stir in 1 tablespoon vinegar or lemon juice.
4. Pour in remaining oil in a slow trickle. Keep whisking. Add remaining vinegar or lemon and water.
5. Taste. Adjust seasoning. Keeps for a week in an airtight container in the fridge.

VARIATION: GARLIC MAYO (ALIOLI) Add 2 crushed garlic cloves at the end.
SEAFOOD MAYO Use all lemon juice, no vinegar. Add 1 crushed garlic clove and a little tomato puree.
CURRIED MAYO Add 2 teaspoons of your best curry paste, 1 crushed garlic clove and a little tomato puree.
JAPANESE MAYO Add wasabi paste – a bit or more to taste.

Pesto

This great sauce multi-tasks. Stir it into pasta or rice. Use in sarnies and tarts. Great with roast and griddled veg. Loves chicken. You'll need loads of basil. Grow your own outside or in a pot on the kitchen windowsill.

Ingredients:
4 oz/100 g fresh basil leaves
5 fl oz/150 ml olive oil
25 g/1 oz pine nuts
2 large garlic cloves
50 g/2 oz Parmesan cheese, grated
Method:
1. Blitz all ingredients, except cheese, in a food processor.
2. Tip into a bowl. Mix in Parmesan. Cover. Chill.
VARIATION: Use coriander or rocket instead of basil.

Garlic bread – a classic

We all love this. It's great with soups, salads, pastas. Bring it on for parties and barbies.

Ingredients:
1 stick French bread
Lots of soft butter
2–3 garlic cloves, crushed
Fresh herbs chopped (optional)
Squeeze of lemon (optional)
Method:
1. Preheat the oven to 200°C/400°F/gas 6.
2. Chuck the butter and crushed garlic into a bowl. Cream together. Mix in herbs and/or lemon, if using.
3. Slash the loaf diagonally, leaving the pieces attached at the bottom. Spread the butter into the cuts.

4. Wrap the bread in foil. Bake on a tray for 25 minutes.

Apple chutney

Apple chutney sorts out your deli foods – pate, cheese. Turns something simple into a feast. Store in recycled jars. Grow an apple tree if you feel like it.

Makes 4 x 900 g/2 lb jars
Ingredients:
2 kg/4½ lb cooking apples
600 ml/1 pint malt vinegar
4 garlic cloves
675 g/1½ lb soft dark brown sugar
125 g/4½ oz stoned dates, chopped
3 teaspoons ground ginger
1 teaspoon ground mixed spice
Large pinch of cayenne pepper
1 teaspoon salt
Method:
1. Peel, core and chop the apples. Tip into a large heavy based saucepan.
2. Add half the vinegar and the garlic. Cook gently, stirring regularly with a wooden spoon till thick.
3. Add the remaining vinegar, sugar, dates, ginger, spice and salt. Cook for 30 minutes, stirring, till thick and sludgy with the odd lump of fruit.

4. Wash jars well. Dry and place on a baking tray. Warm in the oven at 140°C/275°F/gas 1.
5. Ladle into the jars. Put a wax disc from a jam kit directly on the chutney. Dampen a cellophane disc to cover each pot. Secure with an elastic band.
6. Wipe jars while warm. Label when cold. Leave for 2 months before eating.

Baked head of garlic

Makes a great puree for full-on taste. Spread on bread, steak, roast or grilled lamb and chicken. The sort of extra that makes all the difference.

Ingredients:
Whole heads of garlic
Olive oil
Salt
Method:
1. Preheat oven to 220°C/425°F/gas 7. Cut off the very tops of the garlic. Stick in a roasting tin or baking tray.
2. Drizzle with oil. Bake for 30 minutes, till soft. Delicious.

Chicken stock

This is the real thing. Recycle a roast chick and get yourself a great stock. Makes the essential base for soups, stews, risottos, sauces, casseroles and gravy.

Ingredients:
1 roast chicken carcass
2 onions, quartered
1 celery stick, cut into chunks
1 carrot, cut into chunks
1 leek, cut into chunks (optional)
A few fresh herb sprigs, tied with cotton (optional)
Garlic cloves, peeled
3.4 litres/6 pints water

Method:
1. Chuck chicken carcass with any jelly, gravy and meat into a large saucepan.
2. Add the onions, carrot, celery, leek and herbs (if using) and garlic. Pour in the water to cover. The pan should not be too full.
3. Bring to the boil. Skim off any scum. Simmer on low heat for 2–3 hours.
4. Strain stock through a colander over a large bowl. Cool. Cover with cling film. Chill or freeze.
VARIATION: If you haven't got a roast, use chicken portions.

Vegetable stock

Get a load of this into your veggie soups and stews. Use any veg except spuds, turnips and beetroot. Mix and match with the list below.

Ingredients:
2 large onions
1 celery stick
2 leeks
3 carrots
Few black peppercorns
Fresh parsley sprigs
2.3 litres/4 pints water
Juice of 1 lemon
2 garlic cloves
2 teaspoons salt

Method:
1. Wash and roughly chop all the veg. Chuck them into a large saucepan with the other ingredients.
2. Bring to the boil. Half cover. Simmer for 1–2 hours. Strain through a fine sieve.

Shortcrust pastry

Get sorted. Get shortcrust. That's all your pies, tarts, pastry puddings and quiches done. Work really fast. Use cold ingredients and a light touch for a crisp light tasty home-style pastry

For 23 cm/9 in flan tin or 4 small tart tins
Ingredients:
200 g/8 oz plain flour
100 g/4 oz cold butter
2–3 tablespoons very cold water

Method:
1. Sift the flour and salt into a large bowl. Cut butter small. Add to flour.
2. Rub fat into flour lightly with cold fingers till it looks like fine breadcrumbs.
3. Add 2 tablespoons cold water. Mix with a fork till the pastry starts to form. Bring dough together quickly with your fingers. Handle very lightly. Add the remaining water if needed. Wrap in cling film and leave for 20 minutes to chill. Bring back to room temperature.
4. Put dough on a lightly floured board. Roll out with a lightly floured rolling pin.
VARIATION: FOR CHEESE PASTRY At STEP 1, add 50 g/2 oz each of finely grated Parmesan and Cheddar cheese.
FOR SWEET PASTRY At STEP 2, before adding water, stir in 1 tablespoon caster sugar and the grated rind of 1 lemon.

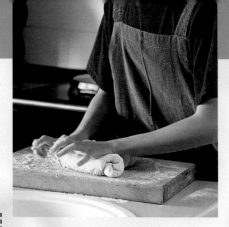

My mum's treacle bread

This bread makes top toast. It's sweet and it's got a great texture. Eat it with anything. Makes any ordinary eat taste really extraordinary. And it's a cheat to make. No kneading. Short rising.

For 2 loaves
Ingredients:
2 tablespoons black treacle
Up to 850 ml/1½ pints warm water
50 g/2 oz fresh yeast
450 g/1 lb strong white flour
450 g/1 lb strong wholemeal flour
1 teaspoon salt
Method:
1. Preheat the oven to 200°C/400°F/gas 6. Grease two 900 g/2 lb loaf tins well.
2. Mix the black treacle with 150 ml/5 fl oz of the water. Crumble in the yeast. Cover with a tea towel. Leave in a warm place for 10 minutes till frothy.

3. Measure flours and sift into a big bowl. Add salt.
4. Make a dent in the flour with a wooden spoon. Tip in yeast mix. Pour in two-thirds of the remaining water and mix well. Then add more water, bit by bit, until you get a soft dough. It mustn't be too sticky or as stiff as regular dough. Use your judgement.
5. Divide the mix between the tins. Pop a carrier bag over the top of each one like a tea cosy. Leave in a warm place to rise for 10–20 minutes. The dough should be just above the tops of the tins.
6. Cook for 30 minutes. Check if the bread is done by turning it out and knocking the bottom of the loaf. Should sound hollow. Pop back in oven for 5–10 minutes if it needs extra.

White loaf

Hmmm – what's best – the crunchy crust or the soft white bread? I can't decide… Your supermarket baker will sort out the fresh yeast. Ask.

For 1 x 900 g/2 lb loaf or 2 x 450 g/1 lb loaves
Ingredients:
25 g/1 oz fresh yeast
1 teaspoon sugar
450 ml/¾ pint warm water
675 g/1½ lb strong white flour
2 teaspoons salt
10 g/½ oz butter
Method:
1. Cream fresh yeast with sugar, add 1 tablespoon of the warm water, and cover. Leave to froth for 10 minutes.
2. Chuck the flour and salt into a large warm bowl. Rub in the butter.
3. Add the fresh yeast mix and the rest of the warm water. Mix with hands or a wooden spoon till you have a firm dough.
4. Throw the dough on to lightly floured surface. Knead well for 8–10 minutes.
5. Put the dough back in the

bowl. Cover with a carrier and leave in a warm place for 1–2 hours, till doubled in size.

6. Grease bread tins well. Preheat the oven to 230°C/450°F/gas 8.

7. Throw dough back on to the floured surface. Knead for 2 minutes. Divide dough for two loaves or leave as one. Put in tins. Cover again. Leave to rise in a warm place until just above the tops of the tins.

8. For a 1 lb loaf bake for about 30 minutes; for a 2 lb loaf bake for about 45 minutes. Turn loaf out and tap the bottom to test if it is cooked – it should sound hollow. Stick it back upside down on the oven shelf without tin if it needs more time. Cool on a rack.

VARIATION: To use fast-action easy blend yeast, add a 7 g sachet to the flour at STEP 2. Follow the rest of the recipe exactly, ignoring the yeast packet's instructions.

Basic white sauce

Essential in best dishes – like cauli cheese, chicken or fish pies, lasagne and pasticcio. Get it smooth and creamy. Once you know how, it's sorted in no time.

Ingredients:
600 ml/1 pint milk
50 g/2 oz plain flour
50 g/2 oz butter

Salt and black pepper
Method:

1. Make a roux: melt the butter gently in a saucepan. Add the flour. Stir quickly with a wooden spoon. Cook for 2 minutes on low heat, stirring so the mix doesn't burn.

2. Take your roux off heat. Add milk slowly – I use a balloon whisk – beating to prevent lumps from forming.

3. Return pan to hob. Increase heat. Bring to the boil and cook for 2 minutes, till sauce thickens, whisking as you go. The sauce is now ready to adapt for your recipe.

VARIATION: BECHAMEL SAUCE Before STEP 1, heat milk with 1 bay leaf, 6 black peppercorns, 1 peeled onion and herbs. Bring to boil. Remove from heat. Leave covered for 10 minutes. Strain through a fine sieve. Use to make the sauce.

Top tip

Cover the surface of a white sauce with greaseproof paper or melt a little butter over it to stop it developing a skin if it's hanging around. Mix butter in before using.

Tomato salad

Essential in our house. Most summer days there's a plate of this. No exact quantities.

Ingredients:
Good ripe tomatoes

Spring onion, chopped or shallot, thinly sliced
Any fresh herb, roughly chopped or torn (optional)
Salad dressing or oil and vinegar or lemon juice
Sea salt and black pepper
Method:

1. Slice your tomatoes on to the plate. Add herbs, spring onion or shallot.

2. Dress and season.

Coleslaw

Good all-year round salad. Trillion times better than shop stuff. No exact quantities. Make it up as you like it.

Ingredients:
Large piece of white cabbage, finely sliced
1 large carrot, coarsely grated
1 small onion, finely sliced
Mayonnaise
Chopped parsley (optional)
Grated rind of 1 orange (optional)
Stoned dates, chopped (optional)
Salt and black pepper
Method:

Mix cabbage, carrot and onion. Add mayo, parsley, orange rind, dates (all if used) and seasoning.

VARIATION:

RED COLESLAW Use red cabbage instead of white.
DRESSED CABBAGE Instead of mayo, use French dressing.

Sam's top 20 tips

1 Get organized. Check ingredients, timings, equipment. Read the recipe right through.

2 Butter burns fast. Add a bit of oil to the pan. Keep the heat low.

3 Add a bit of salt to onions to stop them burning and turning bitter.

4 Get to know your oven. Is it too hot or too cold? Adjust temperatures up or down if you find you need to.

5 Taste your food as you go along through a recipe – how else do you know how it's working out?

6 Use subs if you're missing an ingredient

or two. Get creative.

7 Warm the flour before you start making bread. It helps the yeast.

8 Go easy on salt – a little lifts flavour – a load kills it. Put it in cooking – leave it off the table.

9 Use loads of fresh herbs – they lift out and change flavours. Work out what goes with what. Grow your own.

10 Leave steaks and joints to rest in a warm place after cooking. This maxes the tenderness and flavour.

11 Take risks. Mix weird tastes. Break the rules. Sometimes the best stuff happens when you experiment.

12 Cooking a whole meal? Work it so everything's ready at the same time. Time it. Grab yourself a really loud kitchen timer.

13 Whipping egg whites? These won't whisk up successfully if there's grease on your hands or utensils, or if there's any stray egg yolk.

14 **Cook more than you need.** Eat the next day or freeze – saves time.

15 **Don't get stressed** if things don't go right – work out what went wrong.

16 **Choose your oils well.** Olive is best. Sunflower is good. Use groundnut for curry and sunflower plus sesame oil for stir-fry.

17 **Put your food in the oven** once it's reached the right temperature, not before.

18 **Don't expect home-made food to look and taste like the stuff you buy in.** It'll taste way better, be way cheaper and be different each time you do it which makes it interesting.

19 **Cooking for veggies/vegans/dairy allergies?** Use soy as a dairy substitute. Check the **V** on cheese. Search out other substitutes.

20 **Be an artist on a plate.** Making food look really great is all part of it.

For our family and Purdey

Sam would like to thank: Tom Yule (Yuley), Joe Coulter, Nick Howard, Gareth Dowse (Dowsey), Matthew Ford (Fordy), Jess Taylor, Hattie Coulter, Olivia Towers, Hannah Wilson, Hannah Jackson, Margarete Ousley, Riona Naidu and Daniel Hersi. Thanks also to: Laura Morris for believing in this book, and Denise Johnstone-Burt, Louise Jackson and Barry Timms at Walker Books.

Photographs by Trish Gant

First published 2005 by Walker Books Ltd, 87 Vauxhall Walk, London SE11 5HJ 10 9 8 7 6 5 4 3 2